Agile for Project Managers

Best Practices and Advances in Program Management Series

Series Editor
Ginger Levin

Agile for Project Managers

Denise Canty

CRC Press
Taylor & Francis Group
Boca Raton   London   New York

CRC Press is an imprint of the
Taylor & Francis Group, an **informa** business
AN AUERBACH BOOK

CRC Press
Taylor & Francis Group
6000 Broken Sound Parkway NW, Suite 300
Boca Raton, FL 33487-2742

© 2015 by Taylor & Francis Group, LLC
CRC Press is an imprint of Taylor & Francis Group, an Informa business

No claim to original U.S. Government works

Printed on acid-free paper
Version Date: 20141204

International Standard Book Number-13: 978-1-4822-4498-4 (Hardback)

Visit the Taylor & Francis Web site at
http://www.taylorandfrancis.com

and the CRC Press Web site at
http://www.crcpress.com

I would like to dedicate this book to my husband of several decades, James, our daughter, Raven, our son, Trae-Edward, and our granddaughter, Versailles Isabella-Vision. You guys rock!

This book is also dedicated to my mom, Catherine, my grandma, Jannie, my mother-in-law Mary, and my cousin, Ann. I miss all of you so much.

Finally, I would like to thank my aunt, Rosemary, for all of her prayers.

Contents

Acknowledgments

I give my sincere thanks to Dr. Ginger Levin, who led me down the path of doing what I've always wanted to do, author a book. I will be forever grateful to her for getting me connected.

I also thank my husband, James, for supporting me in everything that I do.

About the Author

Denise Canty is a Project Management Professional (PMP), a PMI Risk Management Professional (PMI-RMP), a Certified Software Quality Engineer (CSQE), and a Certified ScrumMaster (CSM). She holds three degrees from the University of Maryland University College (UMUC):

- Master of Business Administration (MBA), 2013
- Master of Science in IT Project Management (MS), 2012
- Bachelor of Science in Computer Science (BS), 1998

Canty has more than 20 years experience in information technology.

Introduction

This book outlines the agile project management methodology. It represents broad-spectrum agility and does not apply to any one particular method, however, the focus of this book aligns very nicely with the Project Management Institute (PMI) Agile Certified Practitioner (ACP) credential. This book is different because it focuses on the project management component of agility. Focus is put on industry standards, project management, and certifications.

Agility is all about self-directed teams, feedback, light documentation, and working software with short development cycles. Agility is also about values, principles, and terminology, and its popularity is increasing and is here to stay. The role of the project manager with agile differs from traditional project management in that there is minimal up-front planning. This book assists project managers from all industries with the transition to agile project management and indirectly prepares its readers with the basic knowledge needed to pass the PMI-ACP exam.

The highlights of this book are as follows:

- Agile as a project management methodology
- Agile teams
- Agile tools and techniques
- Flavors of agile
- Agile principles
- Agile certifications
- Decision making on which projects should use agile

1

What Exactly Is Agile?

This chapter provides a detailed overview of the meaning of the word "agile" and its relevance to project management. Agility has become an increasingly popular method used to develop products across multiple domains; however, it is envisioned that a clearer understanding of the term can be attained when it is compared to traditional project management concepts.

Agile project management is an approach that is used to design and deliver software. To be exact, the agile approach delivers the software that has the greatest value to the customer. To be *agile* merely means to be quick. The definition of the word is rather easy to understand; however, *quick* is a comparative term used to describe the "degree of comparison between similar adjectives" (i.e., good or better). In other words, the word "quick" is appraised by comparing it to other adjectives with similar meaning with an end result that has the potential to be highly subjective. The assessment of the word "quick" is relative and is based on individualized perceptions. The best way to describe "quick" as it pertains to agile project management is "quicker than traditional project management methods." *Agility* refers to the capability to think and reach conclusions quickly. Traditional project management methods include those that are defined in *A Guide to the Project Management Body of Knowledge (PMBOK® Guide)*, Fifth Edition.[*] PMI describes traditional project management as "being accomplished through the application and integration of the 47 logically grouped project management processes which are then categorized into five Process Groups (i.e., Initiating, Planning, Executing, Monitoring & Controlling, and Closing)." The project management methodology described in the *PMBOK® Guide* is based on a process-oriented

---

[*] Project Management Institute, Inc. (2013).

approach whereas the agile approach is based on values and principles. We now discuss specific high-level reasons why agility has increased in popularity in recent years.

AGILE IS FASTER

Mathematically speaking, it is apparent that traditional project management is not as quick as the agile method with its 47 grouped processes and 5 process groups. In the case of agile, there are 4 values; 12 agile principles; and the Declaration of Interdependence (DOI) for Agile Project Management and its additional principles that tie together "people, projects, and value."* A fact-based determination has just been made from the comparative assessment of the word "quick" as it pertains to the agile description. It has been successfully and objectively determined exactly what "how quick" means based on the number of processes that fall under agile and traditional project management methods, respectively. The lesson to be learned from the assessment is that whenever there is a project that needs to be done quickly, more than likely the agile approach would be best. There are, of course, other factors to take into consideration when deciding on agile or traditional project management. For example, one factor is project size. Additional factors for selecting an agile project are discussed in Chapter 15.

AGILE CHANGES ARE INHERENT

When discussing agility, it is relevant to discuss *change.* That's a word that hardly needs a dictionary lookup. Let's examine the facts: technology always changes; software requirements change and in fact not much in society is constant. The world that we live in is very dynamic. Getting back to software, any information technology software professional will agree that making changes within a traditional software development project at the wrong time can be quite costly. In fact, the costs of software

---

* Griffiths, M. (2012).

changes later in the life cycle are exponentially greater than changes made early on. For example, changes in requirements during the planning phase hardly cost anything; however, once the software code is in production, those changes can be very expensive. Traditional project management is all about plans and planning whereas agility is about adapting and very little or no planning at all. Plans always change because there are a multitude of unknowns in the traditional project management approach. Agile project management adjusts direction on the fly and welcomes change at any time in the project. Keep in mind that we are not referring to just any type of change. We are speaking about those changes that enhance a customer's competitive advantage. It takes time and money to replan and modify project documentation in the traditional project management environment. This would not be the case on the agile project.

AGILE IS VALUE-FOCUSED

The goal of an agile project is to deliver high-value software to the customer as early and as often as possible. To be more specific, we are speaking of business value, which is a driver of agile methods. A project is undertaken by a business so that it increases value in some form, whether it is for increased profits, adherence to government regulations, or for public safety purposes. When making the attempt to move a business in the right direction, choices that need to be made are ones that add the "greatest value" for the business. Thus the agile framework focuses its activities and direction on adding, increasing, or enhancing value for the end user which in turn positively affects the business and its desired goals. One may ask at this point, "How do we evaluate value?" Businesses operate to increase profits. There are objective financial methods that calculate "value." These techniques are used prior to the acceptance of a new project to validate that a project is worthwhile to undertake. Because of the fact that agile projects are "value-driven," results show up early on the project in comparison to traditional project management where it can take considerably longer to see positive results for the business. Why would this be the case? Traditional projects typically evaluate results after the project is completed whereas an agile project uses iterations of working software to measure its levels of progress.

AGILE IS RISK-FOCUSED

Traditional project risk management is very process- and event-driven. In contrast, agile project management risk is controlled through its frequent iterations. As the software proceeds through its iterations, it is easy to detect the point where a risk is encountered. Iterations are tested prior to the introduction of new features and risks can be addressed more quickly as opposed to waiting until all of the code has been completed as in the case of traditional project management. In the case of high-risk user stories, these items are undertaken before less riskier items. Features are added to the code based on the priority level. The higher the priority is, the higher the value and the sooner the feature will be included in the product.

AGILE METHODS SUPPORT THE DELIVERY OF HIGH-QUALITY PRODUCTS

Agile methods support concepts such as *continuous integration* and *sustainable pace* as the basis to ensure that a quality product is delivered. In order to provide consistent value and high quality, the product is continuously developed, tested, and integrated with functionality from the backlog. Maintaining a sustainable pace ensures that there is a healthy balance between work and home life. This leads to consistent accuracy, stability, and quality in the delivery of the product. The development team is required to develop the functionality that has the highest priority from the customer's perspective. The benefit of this approach is that the team has the appropriate amount of time to focus on the quality of the required functionality before anything else.

AGILE MANIFESTO

Agile is all about working code and the procedures used to develop systems quickly. In 2001, several experts got together and decided that they wanted to create a better and faster way to develop code. As a result of this collaboration, the Agile Manifesto was created. The Agile Manifesto is simply a public declaration of intentions. This means that all of the principles, beliefs, and guidelines have been put forth within the Manifesto for Software Development. Keep in mind that agility is not limited to information technology software development. Individuals who work in innovative industries (e.g., engineering), those who transfer information to others (i.e., teaching), and those whose jobs require that they make changes to technology tend to realize the greatest benefits from agility.

TRADITIONAL PROJECT MANAGEMENT

Traditional project management techniques are sufficient for the known aspects of a project but agile methods are better for the unknown and here's why. In order to spend less money on a project, it is necessary to deal in reality. The reality is that up-front planning is often estimated based on prior experience with a similar project. This technique works reasonably well, however, it can be costly at times. According to PMI, a project is a temporary endeavor undertaken to create a unique product, service, or result.[*] Each project has its own uniqueness from other projects. With the agile approach, it is easier and cheaper to adapt to and welcome changes rather than planning the project up front and experiencing a multitude of costly changes through the project. It is well understood that there will always be changes on projects. It is inevitable. See Table 1.1 for a comparison of agile versus traditional project management.

TABLE 1.1

Agile Project Management versus Traditional Project Management

Agile Project Management	Traditional Project Management[a]
Less risk	Increased risk
More visibility	Less visibility
Increased business value	Reduced business value
More adaptability	Less adaptability
Faster software delivery	Slower software delivery
Reduced costs	Increased costs

[a] This is based on the traditional waterfall development model. The waterfall method is sequential where one phase of the life cycle has to be completed before the next phase is started. In contrast, agile methods are iterative and incremental.

[*] PMI. (2013).

MOVING TO AGILE

Many organizations are ready to make the move toward using agile methods. This would require a strategic plan that understands that the transformation is both a social and methodological process. The move to agile methods requires a change in organizational culture because there are many challenges and changes to overcome during the process. Agile methods were created as an alternative to traditional software development methods with promises to deliver software faster, with better quality and higher customer gratification. In order to realize the agile values and principles of the Agile Manifesto (see Chapter 2, "Agile Concepts"), organizations would require across-the-board modifications to their existing software development strategy. A well-developed strategy is required so that any complications and problems encountered are quickly resolved. This way, the amount of implementation time and effort is minimized.

CHAPTER SUMMARY

We will now summarize our discussion on agility and clarify a few known misconceptions.

- The agile approach is not for every project. Chapter 15 goes into greater detail for the reasons behind this statement.
- The agile approach is not better than traditional project management. It is an alternative project management approach.
- Agile methods can increase business profits because they focus more on the portions of the product or service that is the most valuable to the customer. This results in increased business value.
- Agile methods are quicker than traditional project management methods because they are based on values and principles rather than processes and process groups which take longer to execute.
- Agile methods are more adaptive and support change in a less costly fashion than traditional project management.

We are now ready to discuss agile project management in greater detail beginning with Chapter 2. With the agile approach, the project management role is actually shared among three roles: the servant leader, the customer, and the development team. In traditional project management, the project manager's role is usually a demanding balancing act between the project's triple constraints of cost, scope, and schedule.* The benefits of agile are fewer surprises, lower costs, and a more quickly delivered product.

---

* PMI. (2013).

2

Agile Concepts

As discussed in Chapter 1, agile project management is an iterative, adaptable, and collaborative method used to manage the software development process. This chapter examines agile concepts in greater detail. First and foremost, this chapter starts with a discussion of the Agile Manifesto, which is used as the foundation for implementing the agile project. The Agile Manifesto consists of two components: values and guiding principles. Figure 2.1 represents an illustration of the Agile Manifesto.

AGILE VALUES

Agile values represent those items that are valued more than others. Other values refer to those typically used in traditional project management. The reader is again reminded that the agile framework is compared to traditional project management throughout this book. This is done for clarification purposes and because traditional project management was in place long before the Agile Manifesto came about in 2001. A discussion of the four agile values follows.

(a) *Individuals and interactions over processes and tools.* This value statement means that individuals (people) and their interactions have greater value than do processes and tools. Traditional project management places greater emphasis on the utilization of processes and tools. The understanding that needs to be taken from this particular value is that people and the interactions between people are more important than processes and tools. The logic behind this value is that people take on the project (not processes and tools). People do the work and therefore are more valuable.

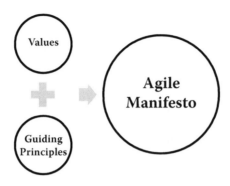

FIGURE 2.1
The Agile Manifesto.

(b) *Working software over comprehensive documentation.* This value statement simply means that working software is more valuable than comprehensive documentation. The Agile Manifesto places greater value on working software because this is what the customer values most. In addition, working software is the main reason that the project has been undertaken. Documentation has its usefulness, however, it has very little value when compared to working software. The customer is paying for software that works and comprehensive documentation is merely a bonus and has little or no value by itself.

(c) *Customer collaboration over contract negotiation.* This value simply implies that collaborating with the customer is more valuable than contract negotiations. Why is this so? This value is based on being flexible as opposed to being rigid and unwavering based on a contract. Traditional project management defines the project scope up front and at times this can be very time consuming and costly to modify. The agile framework supports the changing nature of software requirements, technology, and even the end client. The contracting process on an agile project has to remain more adaptable in comparison with that of traditional project management. There is no formal change management component on the agile project when compared to the traditional project. If a requested change adds value to the project, it is more than likely to be accepted. Negotiating contract changes with the client goes out the door and collaborating with the client to add value to the product is acceptable because it has greater value.

(d) *Responding to change over following a plan.* This value statement implies that it is more valuable to respond to change rather than to follow a plan. With traditional project management and as a result

TABLE 2.1

Agile Value Statements

Agile Value	*Rather Than*	Traditional Value
Individuals and interactions	*Over*	Processes and tools
Working software	*Over*	Comprehensive documentation
Customer collaboration	*Over*	Contract negotiation
Responding to change	*Over*	Following a plan

of changes, it can take considerable time to bring the project back into alliance with the project plan. With agile project management, it is more valuable to respond to project changes rather than adhere to a plan. The agile agenda welcomes and expects project changes. It takes more time to document and approve changes with traditional project management. Although planning on an agile project is minimal, the most valuable actions to take are to respond to change. This is more flexible and faster to do as opposed to following a plan and making changes.

We have covered the four agile values and it is time to recap the important concepts that have been discussed thus far. See Table 2.1 for a consolidated list of the four agile values.

Recap

The Agile Manifesto provides guidance on the agile project based on values that are the most important. As stated in the beginning of Chapter 1, these values are compared with traditional project management values because the author believes this will enhance understanding. Values that are less important on the agile project could possibly coexist with the more desirable values; however, in the case of a conflict, the agile project team must remember and focus on the agile values over the values associated with traditional project management.

AGILE GUIDING PRINCIPLES

As part of the Agile Manifesto and in addition to the four agile values, agile practitioners follow 12 guiding principles. These values and principles are important in gaining the correct understanding of agile project management. Following is a discussion of the agile guiding principles in greater detail.

1. *Our highest priority is to satisfy the customer through early and continuous delivery of valuable software.* The understanding to be gained from this principle is that first and foremost, the goal is to satisfy the customer. How will the customer be satisfied? By the continuous delivery of valuable software. What does valuable software really mean? It refers to software that is valued by the customer. In Chapter 9 of this book we provide a thorough understanding of the term "value" as it applies to agility. Notice the focus on the word *value.* It is a very important word and it represents the main focus of the agile framework. The understanding that must be obtained from this guiding principle is that the agile framework has a customer and a value-based focus.

2. *Welcome changing requirements, even late in development. Agile processes harness change for the customer's competitive advantage.* This guiding principle demonstrates the agile framework's flexibility and adaptability when dealing with change. Traditional project management is generally managed around a change management process and is sometimes viewed as being costly and enabling *scope creep* (i.e., small changes in a plan or project that necessitate other changes which lead to still more changes, etc.). In contrast, the agile process is more accepting of changes at any time, even very late in development. There is no such thing as scope creep in the agile realm because changes are always accepted. If, however, the change does not add value, then there is the possibility that it won't be included in the product. It is important to understand that the focus on the agile project is mainly about value-added changes. The logic behind the acceptance of change is based on several factors:

   • Changes are considered to be the norm on agile projects.
   • Flexibility and adaptability enable and support a customer's competitive advantage by welcoming changes that add value at any time.
   • Accepting change is faster than approving or denying changes. Remember that agility is all about speed! Once again, readers need to understand that only those changes that "add value" are candidates for inclusion into the product. The agile team must

fully understand that they should limit change discussions and actions to value-added propositions only.

3. *Deliver working software frequently, from a couple of weeks to a couple of months, with a preference for the shorter timescale.* Early feedback is decidedly much better than proceeding on a project and getting feedback late. What is worse is that the project could end up heading in the wrong direction. Not only is going down the wrong path quite costly, it is also a great waste of time and effort. An iteration on agile projects should be between two weeks to one month, again with the preference always being the shorter time frame. Why do we want a shorter time frame? There are a couple of reasons:

   • Short delivery cycles result in regular feedback from the project stakeholders. This keeps the project from losing momentum by keeping everyone actively engaged. On a traditional project, slow feedback can result in a lack of engagement by the project team and has the potential to contribute to project delays.

   • Frequent delivery of working software is beneficial in that requirements can be quickly added or modified. Here again, speed is very relevant.

   • How do frequent small changes increase the amount of value-added for the customer? Small and frequent changes can minimize the likelihood that the customer will have the need to create a large number of change requests. This practice ensures that the project is satisfying the customer's requirements on a regular and consistent basis.

   • The goal of the agile project is to deliver value throughout the project. Accepting changes is one practice that supports the goal of consistently adding value to the product.

4. *Business people and developers must work together daily throughout the project.* In order to deliver a project quickly, face-to-face interactions is the fastest way to communicate on agile projects. E-mails, phone calls, and documentation are considered to be less efficient and slower methods of communication. Daily face-to-face interactions between customers and developers enable a faster rate of transferring knowledge. This results in all project stakeholders being on the same page with no surprises. Product delivery on the agile project has a higher rate of success in meeting or exceeding customer expectations based on these interactions.

5. *Build projects around motivated individuals. Give them the environment and support they need, and trust them to get the job done.* Motivated and talented people make a big impact on an agile project. The successful delivery of the product depends on empowered team members. Agile methods are based on self-directed and self-organized teams who can be trusted to get the job done. There is no micromanagement on agile projects. The management style or lack thereof is based on team collaboration. This mind-set results in the project getting completed faster and effectively. The best team members on an agile project are those who can work with little supervision and are self-motivated.

6. *The most efficient and effective method of conveying information to and within a development team is face-to-face conversation.* Such conversations are the fastest way to communicate on agile projects. The flow of communication is more effective and efficient for face to face in comparison with other methods. Inquiries and inconsistencies can be addressed very quickly. This results in minimal delays and faster delivery of the product. Small team sizes make for ease in communicating face to face. In the case of larger project teams, face to face can be challenging, however, the method of communication can be tailored to meet the needs of the project.

7. *Working software is the primary measure of progress.* Progress on the agile project is determined by how well the software works. This is a results-based focus that cannot be easily disputed. Working software shows the customer results that can be approved and accepted. It also shows progress made toward the end goal of product delivery. When the software works, only then can it be approved by the customer as being completed.

8. *Agile processes promote sustainable development. The sponsors, developers, and users should be able to maintain a constant pace indefinitely.* Agile methods support the project team's need to have a life outside of work. This means that the expectation for the team is to maintain a sustainable pace based on a typical 40-hour workweek. Long workdays are not looked upon favorably on agile projects. By working at a sustainable pace, the team can be more productive, which results in less project tension. The sustainable pace is a win–win situation for everyone involved in the project. This in turn is beneficial at the

corporate level in that companies do not want overworked teams who are stressed out, burnt out, and unhappy.

9. *Continuous attention to technical excellence and good design enhance agility.* In order to deliver high value to the end client, it is often necessary for the development team to make changes to the design. This means that the design must be relatively easy to maintain. Technical excellence and a good design make for ease in understanding and making changes to the design. This in turn supports the ability to respond to change very quickly. A good product design and technical excellence enhance agile methods because continuous attention is given to the design of the software. The value of this guiding principle is having a design that is easily maintainable based on its technical excellence.

10. *Simplicity—the art of maximizing the amount of work not done—is essential.* The author believes that this guiding principle is the trickiest one to understand. At face value, the principle talks about work not done. The question then becomes: "Why is there a concern about work not done?" From the agile perspective, work not done is more reliable because there is nothing that could go wrong with it. The development team does not code work that is not done so it's perfect because it has not been touched. It is believed that over 60% of software features are included in a product but are rarely if ever used.* This is the reason why agile methods focus on simplicity. By focusing only on the necessary components of the product, there is less risk. Too much complexity increases project risk. The takeaway of this guiding principle is that simplicity is better than complexity. The development team should only build what is required by the customer. Gold plating (the incorporation of costly and unnecessary features or refinements into a product) is a big no-no. By focusing on simplicity, this in turn speeds up the actual delivery of the product.

11. *The best architectures, requirements, and design emerge from self-organizing teams.* According to agile methods, when people are given the chance to self-manage themselves, they produce better work. This includes the best architectures, requirements, and designs. The best work is developed by those who are the originators of the work. Why is this so? Self-managing teams with the ability to make their own

---

* Griffiths, M. (2012).

decisions take pride in ownership of their work. One reason for this is because these teams are free to work in the manner that suits them without unnecessary interference from others such as the customer and the business people. These teams don't have to sell their ideas to others and this saves a considerable amount of time. Simply put, the agile team is responsible for the outcome of the product and they are the best ones to have the freedom to create it. For clarity, readers need to understand that we are speaking of the development team. This is not inclusive of the customer or the business side of the project.

12. *At regular intervals, the team reflects on how to become more effective, then tunes and adjusts its behavior accordingly.* This guiding principle is simply about lessons learned and when they occur on the agile project. Agile methods support the idea that it is best not to wait until the end of a project to address lessons learned. Lessons learned need to be captured and addressed during the project. For example, in the case of Scrum, lessons learned should be addressed at the end of each Sprint (iteration). Agile methods capture lessons learned as the project ensues rather than at the end of the project. The agile project team then tunes and adjusts its behavior for subsequent iterations. This gives the project team a chance to act on the lessons learned rather than just discussing the actions and hoping for a chance to apply the lessons on future projects.

DECLARATION OF INTERDEPENDENCE

The Declaration of Interdependence (DOI) was developed strictly for the project management side of the agile projects and it is not a part of the Agile Manifesto. As a matter of fact, the DOI was created in 2003, two years after the Agile Manifesto. There are six principles associated with the DOI. According to Griffiths (2012), the DOI is directed at project leadership and is not tested on the PMI-ACP exam.[*] It is important to mention that the difference between the DOI and the Agile Manifesto is that the DOI is for the project management side of an agile project and the latter guides the entire agile project. Following is a discussion of the six principles associated with the DOI.

---

[*] Griffiths, M. (2012).

1. *We increase return on investment by making the continuous flow of value our focus.* This principle means that the agile project provides exactly what the business has asked for and nothing more. The logic behind this principle is that when results are provided that meet the needs of the business, then this makes a case for project continuation and approval. The continuous flow of value means that the project delivers the desired business results instead of simply delivering results that may be useless to the customer.

2. *We deliver reliable results by engaging customers in frequent interactions and shared ownership.* Not only is engaging the customer good business, it helps develop and build relationships. Frequent interactions with the customer support the delivery of a product that meets or exceeds expectations. When the customer is engaged and sharing ownership of the project, the results are undoubtedly reliable.

3. *We expect uncertainty and manage for it through iterations, anticipation, and adaptation.* Agile methods do not rely on plans to guide projects. Change is the expectation for agile methods and it is managed through iterations, anticipation, and adaptation. Software projects are known for constant changes and a good way to manage modifications is to develop software in iterations. The fact that agile methods are highly adaptable means that change is anticipated at any time during the project. The agile project adapts to change for value-added reasons and very little up-front planning is needed.

4. *We unleash creativity and innovation by recognizing that individuals are the ultimate sources of value, and creating an environment where they can make a difference.* Agile methods recognize the value of individuals on the team. The logic behind this principle is that each individual team member must be treated well; his or her needs should be satisfied and each should get the support needed to be successful on the agile project. In addition, the agile project environment should be the best possible one that can be provided.

5. *We boost performance through group accountability for results and shared responsibility for team effectiveness.* Shared responsibility for project success is the idea behind this principle. Self-managed teams are typically more satisfied and enthusiastic when working together to resolve issues. Team empowerment not only results in ownership of project glitches, it encourages team members to work very hard for resolutions. When the entire team shares the responsibility for project success, everyone on the team is a success.

6. *We improve effectiveness and reliability through situational specific strategies, processes, and practices.* It should be well understand that agile methods are flexible and projects are unique. This means that project conditions must be evaluated for the best solutions instead of attempting a one-size-fits-all approach. Based on what is available for the project, agile methods require adaptation for the best solution based on the environment and the circumstances that are present.

CHAPTER SUMMARY

The Agile Manifesto and the Declaration of Interdependence (DOI) represent the foundation for agile methods. There are several main ideas that need to be summarized:

- Agile methods support value-based delivery.
- People on agile projects work on self-directed and self-organized teams.
- Change is welcomed at all times.
- Agile methods are about speed.
- Agile methods support customer collaboration and frequent interactions.
- Agile methods support face-to-face time.
- People should be motivated on the agile project.
- The design should be kept simple and easy to change.
- Agile methods support adaptation on the fly.
- Adequate people skills (soft skills) are particularly important on agile projects.
- Agile methods are about simplicity.
- The software must work or there is no real progress.
- There is a sustainable pace; no long hours.
- Document lessons learned throughout the project; don't wait until the end.

3

The Most Popular Agile Methods

Agile methods have become very popular because of the promise to deliver superior quality products in significantly shorter time frames than traditional practices. Along with meeting an organization's needs and business goals, agile methods focus on satisfying stakeholders and the end user. This chapter discusses two agile methods only: Scrum and XP. There are in fact other agile methods, however, this chapter discusses the two methods that are considered to be the most popular. Additional agile methods are covered in Chapter 17. Scrum and XP are the main agile methods that are covered on the PMI-ACP exam.[*]

Scrum is considered to be a lightweight agile method that uses practices, events, roles, artifacts, and rules for project execution. This method is supported by three "pillars" that guide all facets of the Scrum project:

1. *Transparency:* Everything on a Scrum project is visible to all who have a stake in the outcome.
2. *Inspection:* The Scrum project is inspected on a regular basis to ensure that progress is being made toward the goals and objectives.
3. *Adaptation:* Processes are adjusted as needed when problems or undesirable issues present themselves.

The benefits of Scrum include but are not limited to the following:

- The process is incremental and iterative.
- Requirements are permitted to change over a period of time.
- The end users are actively involved throughout the project.
- The process is straightforward and uncomplicated.

---

[*] Griffiths, M. (2012).

Possible weaknesses of Scrum methods include:

- In the event that a team member leaves the project, the impact is significant.
- The Scrum project requires experienced team members. Inexperienced team members can lead to project delays.
- The method is very informal.

A typical Scrum project has six to ten team members. This agile method is more suited to small teams, however, it can be adapted to large teams as well. Companies and projects that are team, value, and customer oriented are the best candidates for Scrum methods.

XP is considered to be strictly a software development agile method that focuses on good practices. This method supports several core values during its practices. The values are simplicity, feedback, courage, respect, and communication. XP values are manifested throughout the entire life cycle.

The strengths of XP include but are not limited to the following:

- Very responsive to changes
- High priority features are developed first
- Pair programming enhances creativity

Possible weaknesses of XP include:

- Large amounts of overhead may be required.
- The order of feature importance can be subjective.
- XP should not be used on a project with a very large staff.

XP was developed to address the issues associated with project risk. XP practices were established to mitigate risk and increase the probability of success. XP was developed for small groups of developers (i.e., between 2 and 12). Risky project types that are good candidates for XP include but are not limited to the following:

- The customer needs a new system by a certain date.
- A new system is a big challenge for the software industry as a whole.
- A new system is a challenge for a company's internal software group.

We now begin our discussion with an overview of Scrum. Figure 3.1 outlines the Scrum process in detail.

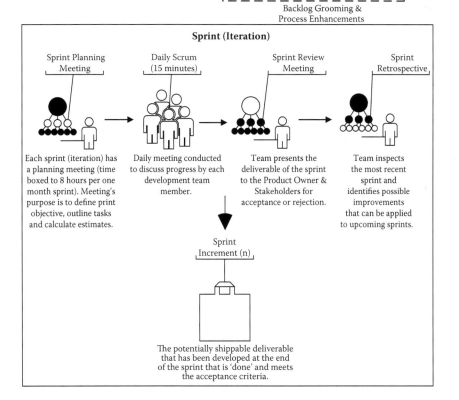

FIGURE 3.1
Scrum process.

SCRUM OVERVIEW

Scrum is a lightweight agile framework used for developing a product. For the purposes of our discussion, we need to clarify what we mean by the word *product*. A product is typically software when we are referring to development work; however, a product can be a service, a tangible deliverable, or a desired result. According to SCRUMstudy (2013)*, the Scrum framework can be used on any type of project in any industry. This means that Scrum can be effective on small as well as large teams upward of hundreds of team members. In the case where the Scrum team size is larger than ten, it is recommended that several Scrum teams be formed. For the purposes of this book, the author's focus is on small teams with at least six to ten members.

The work on a Scrum project is divided into *Sprints* (iterations). The team on a Scrum project is self-directed, cross-functional, and is empowered to make its own decisions. At the end of each Sprint, the Scrum team creates a potentially deliverable product (*Sprint increment*). The Scrum framework delivers products based on empirical process control (observing and experimenting) rather than up-front project planning. In order for the Scrum project to deliver the best value to the customer as quickly as possible, the team must prioritize and determine what should be done. All stakeholders on the Scrum project collaborate, interact, and work in a cohesive fashion in order to deliver the greatest amount of product value. In addition, time-boxing is a Scrum technique that establishes the time frames under which work is completed and meetings are conducted.

The Scrum framework is very adaptable based on the fact that very little up-front planning is done and the focus is on observing and doing. The product's development is iterative, very flexible, and designed to incorporate changes at any point in the project. The information path on the project is very open and transparent where everyone can quickly and easily see the status. The Scrum team gets continuous feedback as a result of meetings and activities. Each Sprint provides the team with an opportunity for continuous improvement with the product and the team's practices. The iterative nature of Scrum provides for frequent delivery of the product based on the customer's needs which in turn translates to continuous value for the customer. The Scrum framework is based on working under a

---

* SCRUMstudy. (2013).

sustainable pace for an indefinite amount of time and typically this would mean that the workweek is 40 hours per week maximum.

The *product backlog*, a requirements document that represents the project scope, is prioritized based on the product features that have the greatest amount of value for the customer. To be clear, the customer is responsible for making the determination as to which requirements are considered to be the high-value ones. High-value requirements are delivered earlier than those with lesser value. The Scrum development process is considered to be very efficient in that most of the activities are *timeboxed*. This means that a short and specific period of time is established for the work to be completed. This leads to an efficient development process for the Scrum project. The Scrum framework is reported to lead to very high levels of team motivation, namely because of the daily standup meetings and Sprint retrospective processes. The Sprint team can resolve problems faster than with traditional project management because of colocation, collaboration, and cross-functional teams. Scrum deliverables are deemed more effective because of regular customer interactions and the prioritized backlog based on the customer's needs. There is a heavy focus on increasing business value by collaboration with stakeholders under a customer-focused framework.

Scrum processes facilitate a high trust environment with very little conflict among team members. This occurs because of the *daily standup meetings* (15-minute time-boxed discussions used to report progress), and *Sprint retrospectives* (meetings used to discuss lessons learned during the end of each iteration) that promote Scrum principles such as openness, collaboration, and face-to-face communication. In addition, the Scrum work environment is one where team members are permitted to take ownership of the project work, resulting in a high quality product. Everyone is responsible together for the success of the project and product delivery. A collaborative work environment enables the Scrum team to attain a very high velocity. Finally, working under an innovative environment has the potential to increase learning, adaptability, and contemplation. An innovative environment has a high probability of an increase in the level of creativity in the work environment.

Scrum Transparency

Scrum activities are very transparent in that all project-related information is visible to all stakeholders and project team members. Information flows very freely and is not hidden from anyone on the team. All team members are made aware of the project vision; the product backlog is posted for everyone to see; the progress of the team is discussed out in the open during the daily Scrum meeting and everyone is made aware of release plans. In addition, Sprint review meetings include everyone and Burndown and Burnup Charts reflecting the amount of work that has been accomplished are posted for viewing by all.*

Adaptation

Adaptation is a Scrum concept that refers to flexibility based on the needs of the project. The Scrum team learns what needs to be accomplished almost effortlessly as a result of the project's transparency. By monitoring and observation, the team is able to adapt as required by making improvements to the work as needed. There is very little planning on Scrum projects because of adaptation. As a result of adaptation, the finished product has a very high probability of success.

The Scrum team utilizes information obtained from the following sources for adaptability:

- *Daily Standup Meetings:* A 15-minute time-boxed meeting where team members come together to discuss progress.
- *Retrospect Project Meetings:* A meeting used to determine how collaboration and effectiveness of the Sprint team can be improved in the future.
- *Retrospect Sprint Meetings:* A four-hour time-boxed meeting used to discuss lessons learned throughout a Sprint.
- *Consistent Risk Identification and Management:* As a result of regular feedback, risks are discussed during the daily meetings and are addressed during the upcoming Sprint.
- *Change Requests:* Small changes are approved by the Product Owner. Any requested change that cannot be approved by the Product Owner is presented to the stakeholders. If the change is significant, then senior management must provide the approval. Changes are also approved during the grooming of the product backlog.
- *Scrum Principles and Values:* Values are identified in this chapter under the heading "Core Values of Scrum." Scrum principles are outlined in Table 3.1.

---

* SCRUMstudy. (2013).

TABLE 3.1

Comparison of Scrum and XP

	Scrum (Project Management Approach)	XP (Software Development Methods)
Objective	Communication Team and management interactions Team empowerment	The customer has the driver's seat The code is the main focus
Perceptions	High-value focused Risk focused Team controlled	Trust the developers to get the job done Developers can "Do their thing" Lack of management control
Principles	Commitment Servant leadership Openness Respect Courage Self-organizing project teams Multifaceted knowledge transfer Subtle control Regular transfer of information Visibility Communications No interference	Quick feedback Incremental change Excellence in work Common understanding Programmer well-being Continuous process Communication Simplicity Courage Initiative
Motivation	Identify changes early Let the development team do their job and stay out of their way	Refactoring the code makes it easy to change Customer has authority to make all business decisions Development team has the authority to make all technical decisions Short iterations Customer provides fast feedback
Activities	Sprint planning Daily Scrum Sprint review Retrospectives	Create user stories Release planning Planning games Code development Spikes Execute Acceptance Tests

continued

TABLE 3.1 (continued)

Comparison of Scrum and XP

	Scrum (Project Management Approach)	XP (Software Development Methods)
Roles	ScrumMaster	Programmer
	Product owner	Customer
	Scrum team	Coach
		Tracker
		Sponsor
		Manager
Deliverables	Sprint backlog	Release plan
	Release backlog	User stories
	Product backlog	Product backlog
		Unit tests
		Acceptance test
Approach	Iterative incremental	Iterative incremental
Iteration length	2–4 weeks	1–3 week iterations
Planning	Iteration planning	Planning games
Artifacts	Release planning	Stories
	The finished product (operational)	Constraints
		Tasks
		Acceptance tests
		Code
		Releases
		Metaphors
		UML design
		Documentation
		Standards
		Unit tests
		Planning
		Release plans
		Iteration plan
		Test results
		Spike solutions
		Resources
		Scope
		Quality
		Time
		Tracking results
Project Type	Small projects	Quick development
		Not dependent upon a deadline
Scope	Defined by the customer	Uses a product backlog to define scope

TABLE 3.1 (continued)

Comparison of Scrum and XP

	Scrum (Project Management Approach)	XP (Software Development Methods)
Practices	Create product backlog	Planning games
	Identify and remove impediments	Small releases
		Simple design
	Define Sprint backlog	Metaphors
	No interference allowed	Refactoring
	No intruders allowed	Testing
	Demonstrations	Pair programming
	Observations	Collective code ownership
		Continuous integration
		40-Hour workweek
		On-site customer
		Coding standards

Source: Derived from G. Admad, T. R. Soomro, and M. N. Brohi, *European Academic Research,* 2014. Retrieved from http://www.euacademic.org/UploadArticle/273.pdf. With permission.

Inspection

This Scrum concept is based on the team having visible information sources available for inspection. The Scrum board (see Table 3.2), a tool used for Scrum planning and tracking purposes, shows the team's progress for the completion of tasking for the current Sprint. The customer, the person or company that procures the project's product, services, or result, provides constant feedback with regard to the prioritization of the product backlog items, breaking down *epics* (i.e., large untouched user stories), and release planning activities. Finally, an inspection is performed to validate the product at the end of each Sprint. Inspection is a way to verify quality and provide the customer an opportunity to inspect the product for acceptance.

TABLE 3.2

Scrum Board

To Do	Work in Progress	Done	Sprint Goal
Story Story Story Story	Story Story Story	Story Story Story	Burndown Chart

Iterative and Incremental Development

This refers to a style of product development that is done in iterations and is focused on improving the product over a period of time. An important aspect of iterative development is that it provides opportunities for rapid feedback used to decide the next steps for the product's features. High-priority functionality is iteratively added to the product and changes are effectively addressed, one iteration at a time. Scrum is also considered to be incremental, which means that new features are added to the existing code. In contrast, iterative development refers to making modifications to existing functionality. Thus the product is both incrementally and iteratively developed.[*]

Time-Boxing

This is an agile concept that refers to fixed periods of time for work to be finished and for activities such as meetings to take place. When the established time has expired, the event is discontinued and whatever has not been completed is moved to the next time-boxed period. An example of a time-boxed event is the daily standup meeting which is set for 15 minutes per day. Sprints are time-boxed at two weeks or up to a month.

Collaboration

With Scrum, this is a concept that refers to product development that includes all stakeholders collaboratively working together to create and deliver the high possible amount of value. We recall the agile principle: *"Customer collaboration over contract negotiation."* Collaboration must occur in order to develop and deliver the product increments that have the maximum amount of value for the customer. In cases where requirements need to be better understood, collaborating with the customer minimizes the need for excessive change requests. In addition, as threats appear on the project, customer collaboration can result in the early identification and assessment of uncertainty, which in turn lessens the overall risk impact for the project as a whole. The customer is the best resource, in most cases, to address issues with user stories (requirements).

---

[*] Griffiths, M. (2012).

Self-Organization

The expectation for a successful outcome on a Scrum project is that the team is self-motivated and accepts full responsibility for the success of the product. When the team is also self-organized, then the expectation is that a high-value product will be delivered. Scrum projects work under the "servant leadership" principle where the needs of the team are satisfied in order to achieve the desired product results.

It must be made clear that a self-organizing team does not have the right to do whatever it wants to do. This means that team members use their own judgment and experience to get the work done on the project based on the technical and managerial requirements necessary to deliver the product. Each member of the Scrum team takes responsibility for defining and completing tasks, creating estimates, and agreeing upon the team's velocity during the Sprints.

Scrum Management and Leadership Styles

On the Scrum project, the role of the project manager is considered to be distributed. This means that project management functions are "shared" among the Product Owner, the ScrumMaster, and the Scrum team. On traditional project management teams, the project manager has responsibility for the majority of the leadership and management tasks. In contrast, the ScrumMaster functions as a servant leader to the Scrum team, ensuring that the path is clear so that the product to be delivered has high value for the customer. The Scrum team self-organizes and self-manages with minimal interference and obstacles along the way. Lastly, the team collaborates with the customer on a consistent basis. Up-front planning is practically nonexistent.

Scrum Roles and Responsibilities

Scrum roles consist of three types: the development team, the Product Owner, and the ScrumMaster. Ancillary or additional team members include stakeholders who give advice, support the team, and are watchful of the project. To add humor and fact to this discussion, the core team includes the Product Owner, developers, and the ScrumMaster and the group is considered to be the pig. The ancillary team, the project stakeholders are referred to as the chicken.[*] All team members must come into agreement with regard to what "done" actually means for the project. A discussion of each role follows.

Product Owner

The Product Owner is considered to be the customer or the voice of the customer. The responsibilities of the Product Owner include the following:

- Creates the product vision for team and stakeholder acceptance
- Accepts or rejects the product increment at the end of each Sprint
- Prioritizes requirements (user stories) in the product backlog based on business value
- Clarifies items in the product backlog
- Establishes release dates for the product
- Assesses the feasibility of the product
- Overall responsibility for the product delivery
- Ensures that the product backlog is transparent on the project
- Establishes the goal for each Sprint
- Grooming of the product backlog
- Obtaining the maximum business value
- The Product Owner also shares the Servant Leader role with the ScrumMaster

ScrumMaster

The ScrumMaster's role on the team is that of a facilitator, motivator, and coach. The responsibilities of the ScrumMaster include:

- Protecting and guarding the team from outside interferences
- Not conducting any actual technical work
- Making sure that the team follows the Scrum procedures
- Functioning as a change agent; making sure that the change process is obstacle and hassle free
- Maintaining the *Blocks List* (the list of impediments and unresolved issues encountered by the team)
- Servant Leader to the Scrum team

---

[*] SCRUMstudy (2013).

Scrum Team

The Scrum team (i.e., the development team) is self-managing, cross-functional, and consists of six to ten members on average. The responsibilities of the Scrum team include:

- Completing the work on the product during Sprints
- Understanding the requirements
- Maintaining equality among all team members
- Being generalists across domains and specialists in a minimum of one area
- Grooming of the product backlog with the Product Owner

SCRUM PLANNING

The Scrum framework has several planning events (meetings) to establish the goals for each Sprint. A discussion of these important activities follows.

Sprints

A Sprint is a time-constrained (time-boxed) iteration of two weeks to one month used to build a potentially shippable product increment. Each Sprint is implemented similar to a small project and it consists of five major milestones:

- *Daily Scrum:* A daily 15-minute time-boxed meeting used for the development team members to discuss progress, issues, and provides answers to three important questions:
  1. What have I completed since the last meeting?
  2. What will I do before tomorrow's meeting?
  3. What, if any, obstacles are in my way?
- *Sprint Review:* A meeting that is conducted at the end of every Sprint to present the product increment to the Product Owner and stakeholders. Backlog items are presented for acceptance; however, these items can in fact be rejected by the Product Owner.
- *Sprint Retrospective:* A lessons learned meeting conducted at the end of every Sprint. The meeting is based on the previous Sprint and opportunities for improvement of future Sprints are discussed.

- *Sprint Planning Meeting:* A time-boxed eight-hour meeting (per one month Sprint) that takes place at the start of every Sprint. The purpose of this meeting is to establish objectives and estimates for completing tasks. The product backlog is broken down into tasks. Estimates are created for the tasks in terms of complexity, risk, and completion times. All tasks defined in the Sprint planning meeting are included in the Sprint backlog.
- *Release Planning Meeting:* A meeting used to establish the durations of the Sprints and the planning for multiple Sprints within a release. In other words, the purpose of a release planning meeting is to establish the schedule for the product releases.

CORE VALUES OF SCRUM[*]

The Scrum Alliance promotes and acknowledges a solid foundation of values for the Scrum team's processes and main beliefs. These five core values provide the team guidance that focuses on collaboration and continuous improvement.

1. *Focus.* The team's focus is only on a small amount of things at a time. The team works well together to create superior work. Value is delivered sooner rather than later.
2. *Courage.* The team members are all in it together. They are not alone. They have support and resources at their disposal. They have the courage to take on great challenges.
3. *Openness.* Team members all work together as one team. They communicate and openly express themselves on progress and obstacles. They openly address any concerns they may be having.
4. *Commitment.* Team members are committed to having control over their destiny. They are committed to the team's success.
5. *Respect.* The team members work well together because they share successes and failures. They respect each other and in turn they are worthy of being respected.

---

[*] Scrum Alliance (2013).

SPRINT ARTIFACTS (DELIVERABLES)

There are several artifacts associated with the Scrum framework. A discussion of the particular items that must be established and delivered for the project follows.

Product Vision

The product vision is a single sentence that describes the expectations for the product. This statement is created by the Product Owner and is agreed upon by the Scrum team.

Prioritized Product Backlog

This artifact is a list of product requirements (i.e., user stories) that are implemented as product features and functionality. Items in the product backlog support the delivery of the product vision. The Product Owner owns the product backlog and has the responsibility for prioritizing the items on the list based on value.

Sprint Goal

The Sprint goal is presented by the Product Owner and represents the goal(s) for the current Sprint.

Sprint Backlog

The Sprint backlog represents the list of requirements that have been assigned to a particular Sprint. The development team commits to completing all items in the Sprint backlog. The Sprint backlog includes a list of estimated tasks that only the development team can change. To be clear, only the development team can change the *tasks* within a Sprint. The Sprint backlog items cannot be changed once agreed upon by the team. The product backlog must be "groomed." This is a process of adding additional detail and organization to the backlog. The Product Owner and the developers take responsibility for grooming the backlog. Developers may update task estimates and the Product Owner may change the priority of the backlog items.

Blocks List

The blocks list represents any obstacles and outstanding issues that the development team may be facing. This list is addressed and maintained by the ScrumMaster for resolution.

Sprint (Product) Increment

This is the potentially deliverable product increment created by the development team that will satisfy acceptance criteria.

Sprint Burndown Chart

This chart is used by the Scrum team to track the progress of the Sprint. Stakeholders use this chart to determine how much work remains (*y*-axis) to be completed in the Sprint, based on the amount of time remaining in the Sprint (*x*-axis). The chart shows the velocity (speed) of the team when completing the work for the product. On a daily basis, the team updates this chart based on the work that has been completed. The chart also provides an indication of whether the team will complete all of the planned work in a Sprint. The Planned versus Actual lines indicate how well the Sprint is proceeding according to the team velocity. Figure 3.2 represents a sample Sprint Burndown Chart.

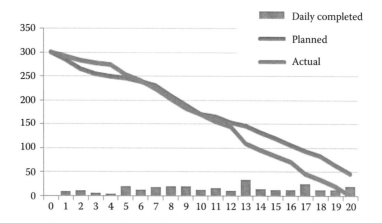

FIGURE 3.2
Burndown Chart example.

Scrum Board

The Scrum team utilizes a whiteboard to plan and track its progress during a Sprint. The Scrum board has three columns that illustrate the progress of the Sprint (To Do, Work in Progress, Done). In addition, the Scrum board also displays the Scrum Burndown Chart. Table 3.1 shows an example of a Scrum board and the Burndown Chart.

Recap of Scrum

The Scrum framework's most important factors are: [*]

- Scrum projects are completed in iterations (Sprints).
- Scrum is more of a project management focused agile method in comparison with other methods.
- High business value functionality has the top priority level for completion.
- Each Sprint produces a potentially deliverable product increment subject to the Product Owner's approval.
- Regular interactions occur between the customer and the Scrum team. This would include the Scrum meetings: Daily Standup, Sprint Planning, Sprint Review, and Release Planning.
- Face-to-face interaction promotes speed in communication.
- Working software at the end of each Sprint is the measure of success.
- Everyone on the team is equally responsible for the success of the project.
- Changes in the product requirements are easily accommodated and expected.
- The Scrum framework ensures that progress is made on a continuous basis.

We now move our discussion to the next agile method: XP (Extreme Programming).

EXTREME PROGRAMMING (XP) OVERVIEW

Extreme Programming or XP is an agile method that is focused on software development best practices. XP was developed by Ken Beck, a software

---

[*] SCRUMstudy (2013).

engineer, during the 1990s. XP was created to be a software development discipline used to create high-quality software more productively.[*] Scrum and XP are methods that use iterations, however, Scrum iterations last two to four weeks and XP iterations last for one to two weeks. XP is very strict with working in priority order, however, Scrum developers have decision making authority to determine how backlog items will be turned into tasks. Lastly, Scrum can be used with large teams, but XP teams need to be small so that they can operate efficiently and effectively.

XP Core Values[†]

The core values for XP include the following:

1. *Simplicity.* The development team does only what is required and nothing more. This keeps things simple and value is maximized. Baby steps are taken in order to reach goals and mitigate failures when they occur. The team creates work they are proud of and the work is maintainable for the long term at reasonable costs.
2. *Communication.* The development team communicates face to face on a daily basis. The team works together on every single thing and creates the best possible solution together.
3. *Feedback.* The team uses all iterations to deliver working software on a frequent basis. The team listens and makes changes very carefully. The team talks about the project together and adapts processes as required.
4. *Courage.* Team members are truthful when discussing progress and estimates. They do not document or make any excuses for failure because they have courage. They have no fear because they work together. They adapt to changes at any time when they occur.
5. *Respect.* Everyone gives and receives respect on the team. Everyone is valued as a team member. The development team respects the knowledge of the customer and vice versa. The management team respects the team's rights to accept responsibility and for them to have authority over their own work.

---

[*] Wells, D. (2013a).
[†] Wells, D. (2013b).

XP Roles and Responsibilities

The XP team has several roles on its projects: customer, developer, tracker, and coach. The first two roles are core and the remaining two are supplementary and may not be present on every XP project. A discussion of each role follows.

Customer

The customer defines the requirements for the project and establishes the project goals. In addition, the customer makes the hard business decisions for the project and works very closely with the software developers. The more involved the customer, the higher the likelihood of project success on an XP project. In actuality, the customer is the voice of the end user of the product. This role clarifies the features of the product and writes the user stories for the team. Finally, this role executes customer tests with assistance from the development team to ensure that a user story is actually done. The working software at any time on an XP project should include all functionality that has the greatest value to the customer.

Developer

The responsibility of the developer on an XP project is to create product functionality based on the user stories provided by the customer. This role must understand and implement product features by working very closely with the customer. Tasks are created from user stories and correct estimates enable the customer to decide which user stories have the highest priorities. Developers are empowered to estimate their own tasks without any interference from the customer.

Tracker

This role is considered to be supplementary and does not exist on every XP project. The tracker is responsible for maintaining the project schedule. Team velocity is also measured and tracked by this role. Regular tracking of the team's progress enables adjustments to be made that will ensure that iterations stay on target.

Coach

The coach is another supplementary role that may not exist on every XP project. This role is responsible for providing guidance and team mentoring. The coach's role is to ensure that the team understands the XP practices in conjunction with software development. This role also assists with problem solving and functions as an arbitrator between the customer and the development team if needed.

XP Core Practices

The XP methodology has several core practices that are considered to be best practices for agile software development. A discussion of these practices follows.

1. *Whole Team.* This XP practice ensures that the "whole team" sits together in the same location for the duration of the project. This refers to everyone, specifically the customer and the development team. The reason for this practice is to ensure ease in sharing information. XP supports the idea of generalizing specialists on its projects. This means that anyone who is qualified for a role can take it on because XP roles are not limited to people who have specialized skills in a particular area. This practice is popular because it enables team members who can perform multiple roles to switch back and forth from one role to another on demand. This practice also keeps everyone on the team engaged while working to ensure a balanced work load.

2. *Planning Games.* The XP planning games practices have two major events: release planning and iteration planning. A release represents a software version with new functionality that is delivered to the production end user. Releases typically occur once or twice a year. Iterations, however, represent short development cycles that occur every two weeks for XP projects and are included within a release.

3. *Small Releases.* The XP practice of small releases means that software is delivered to the test environment to show that the software is working. As we know from Scrum, working software is an indication of progress. Small releases support a quality product and extensive testing is conducted by means of continuous integration of the software.

4. *Customer Tests.* The XP customer defines the actual tests that show that the software is actually working. The development team constructs the test per the customer requirements to verify that the software is in fact working as it should.

5. *Collective Code Ownership.* This XP practice means that any pair of developers is authorized to modify any part of the code on the project. Multiple people may work on the code and this is expected to result in increased visibility and knowledge of the code among the development team. With multiple eyes on the code, this practice ensures that the code is of high quality because defects can be better detected. In the event that a developer leaves the project, the impact will be lessened because knowledge of the code has been previously shared.

6. *Code Standards.* In order to practice collective code ownership on an XP project, it is necessary for all developers to follow a code standard to ensure that the code looks as if a single person has made the changes. No specific code standard is required, however, all developers must be consistent with the method of writing code.

7. *Sustainable Pace.* XP understands that the team must maintain a consistent level of productivity. This can only be accomplished if the team maintains a sustainable pace which translates into a 40-hour workweek.

8. *Metaphor.* XP uses metaphors to reach a common understanding of designs and to establish a shared technical vision. A *metaphor* is something used to represent something else. For example, a metaphor is: the address module is like a GPS that makes sure the locations are correct.

9. *Continuous Integration.* This practice refers to the integration of the code and making sure that all of the code works well together. The practice is important because problems can quickly be detected before integrating defective code or mismatched design. Continuous integration ensures that integration testing is conducted on the code every time new functionality is added. This results in problems being detected immediately.

10. *Test-Driven Development.* This practice requires that the team write the test before developing the code. This means that in order to show that the developed tests work correctly, the code is expected to fail the first time the tests are run. Once the functionality has been correctly

developed, the tests will then pass to show that the code has been written correctly. The idea behind test-driven development is that the test and feedback cycle is as short as possible so that the feedback can occur early.

11. *Refactoring.* This XP practice is a process of enhancing the code's design without changing the functionality. The design should always be efficient where adding changes is easy. Refactoring removes duplicate code, increases cohesion, and decreases dependency among code modules.

12. *Simple Design.* XP supports simple design where the development team can quickly and easily make changes. The design should remain simple in that only the simplest things that work are included with no complicated structures or features. Design complexity increases risk and has historically resulted in failed projects.

13. *Pair Programming.* XP practices require that two developers (a pair) work on the code at the same time. This results in dynamic reviewing of the code at all times. This saves time because issues can be detected very early and it is beneficial to have two developers share the same knowledge of the code.

Recap of XP

We now provide a recap of XP.

- Developers are empowered to respond to changes at any time in the life cycle.
- XP is focused on teamwork to accomplish its goals.
- XP is a software development focused agile method.
- The customer drives the XP project and must always be available.
- Design is kept simple at all times.
- Feedback is provided early and continuously.
- Iterations are typically two weeks long.
- Software is delivered in small releases.

CHAPTER SUMMARY

We will now conclude this chapter by providing factors to consider when selecting either of the two most popular agile methods: Scrum and XP. Table 3.2 provides a side-by-side comparison of the two methods. When making a decision to use XP or Scrum, the project manager may want to select XP for web-enabled projects that require very little documentation and are restricted on their time to market. XP was designed to reduce the overhead associated with project management. With regard to Scrum, this method is more project management focused than XP. In addition, Scrum is more product focused than XP. We hope this information is helpful when making a decision upon which method to choose. Keep in mind that there are many more agile methods from which to select. The agile method selection process should be based on the needs of the organization or the project requirements.

This concludes our discussion on two different agile methods, Scrum and XP. Chapter 17 provides a discussion of additional agile methods.

4

Agile Tools

This chapter discusses the types of tools that are used on agile projects. These tools enhance a team's performance and improve communication and collaboration. Simple tools rather than those that are complex are better suited for agile projects. It is a well-known fact that tools which take a considerable amount of time to master are often considered to be confusing and complex. The agile framework is based on simplicity and tools that have a negligible amount of complexity are more desirable. Our discussion begins with agile project management tools at a very high level. The author does not endorse or recommend any particular type of tool and is merely providing information as to how to select the best agile project management tool based on organizational requirements.

AGILE PROJECT MANAGEMENT TOOLS

Agile project management tools or *agile product management* tools are used to manage the agile project from the beginning to the end by assisting with the creation of the product's vision to the actual delivery of the product. It is important to note that many of these tools are geared toward the Scrum framework rather than generic agile principles. This may be attributable to the current popularity of Scrum and, as of 2014, it being the most commonly used agile method. The majority of the agile project management tools are web enabled. This is as expected because web-enabled technology encourages team collaboration. Agile project management tools are designed for the creation and maintenance of the prioritized product backlog, for iteration and team velocity tracking, and for creating user stories. These are just a few of the tools' most common features and most, if not all, have the capability to address all components of the Scrum framework.

The agile project management tool market is expanding remarkably well, however, this has not made the tool selection process simple enough for many companies who want to embrace the agile framework. In order to identify the appropriate tools, it is recommended that the following analysis and review techniques be conducted in order to select the best tools based on the needs of the organization.

Tools Review and Analysis Process

First, it is recommended that information on only a few tools be carefully studied, analyzed, and evaluated for suitability and budgetary constraints. During the author's analysis of agile project management tools on the Internet, it was very quickly discovered that the information provided was not detailed enough, lacked objectivity, and was based only on the perceived popularity of the selected tools. Basically, there was no identified rational basis for the selection of the agile tools other than what appeared good enough for selection.*

Second, the needs of the project or organization must be established. In order to accomplish this step, it is necessary to study the firm's products, agile processes, and any related documentation. It is basically a sound idea to compile a list of attributes that the team desires to have in an agile tool. Although highly subjective, user-friendliness is an important feature and should be taken into serious consideration based on the perceptions of the team. Be advised that this process may not be a simple task because the agile team's roles may add complexity into the needs analysis process.

Third, the process must include an examination of the agile project management tools available in the marketplace. During this step, the company must select several tools for the review process. The selection process should be based on a number of factors such as:

1. Interest levels of the company
2. Popularity of the tool
3. Level of support for agile methods at the company
4. Integration of the selected tool with the company's existing systems

---

* Azizyan, G., Magarian, M., and Kajko-Mattsson, M. (2012).

5. Licensing requirements
6. Platform under which the tools will perform
7. The company's agile management processes

The recommended number of tools for evaluation should not be greater than three or four, however, some companies may choose to evaluate many more based on direction from senior management.

Fourth, the selection of tools for review must be carefully evaluated prior to purchasing. Evaluation factors are those identified attributes from Step two. In addition, the attributes should be ranked based on their level of importance to the agile team or organization. An example of agile project management tool attributes and weighted scores are shown in Table 4.1. It is important to note that the attributes in the author's list are subjective. The actual attributes that are chosen in this step should reflect the needs of the organization.

Fifth, it is recommended that a survey be conducted with questions that can provide insight into what the actual agile teams specifically need with regard to a tool. A survey can reveal what the company believes is relevant to their agile processes and fill in any gaps in information from the previous steps. Several possible survey questions are identified in Table 4.2.

TABLE 4.1

Possible Agile Project Management Tool Attributes and Ranks

Attribute	Score (1–5)	Rank (1–5)	Weighted Score (Score × Rank)
User friendliness	5	5	25
Backlog	4	3	12
Iterations	2	5	10
User stories	1	1	1
Remote capability	5	3	15
Status tracking	4	5	20
Search capability	1	3	3
Burndown charts	1	4	4
Task tracking	5	5	25
Estimates	5	2	10
Vision	5	1	5
Planning capability	5	2	10
Graphs	5	4	20

TABLE 4.2

Survey Questions for the Agile Project Management Tool Selection Process

Number	Question
1	How do you work with the current agile project management system?
2	What do you like in the existing system? Are you pleased with this system?
3	What improvements do you need in the new system?
4	What do you want to change in the new system?
5	Is there anything that is making your job difficult in the present system?
6	What are your must haves?

TABLE 4.3

Analysis of Agile Project Management Tool Results

Attribute	Tool 1	Tool 2	Tool 3	Tool 4	Tool 5	Tool 6
User friendliness	10	25	5	12	6	5
Backlog	6	4	5	6	10	10
Iteration	8	9	8	9	9	9
Management	10	6	6	8	8	8
User stories	9	9	9	9	9	9
Remote	9	9	9	9	9	9
Status tracking	8	8	8	8	9	9
Search capability	9	20	8	5	5	5
Charts	9	9	10	8	8	8
Burndown/burnup	5	5	5	5	5	5
Task tracking	6	6	6	4	4	4
Estimates	3	8	9	10	8	8
Vision	5	8	8	9	9	9
Planning	5	25	9	9	9	9
Graphs	6	8	9	5	8	8
Total Rating	98	159	114	116	116	115
Average Rating	**6.5**	**10.6**	**7.6**	**7.7**	**7.7**	**7.7**

The final step is to analyze the results. This would be based on the attributes of the tools and their relevance of importance (rank). Table 4.3 shows an example of how the analysis of the attributes might be presented. Again, the tool should be selected based on how well it fits the needs of the organization. This would be based on the scoring of attributes that have been deemed to be important. The higher the average rating, the more relevant are the tools' attributes in meeting the needs of the organization.

Keep in mind that after conducting the analysis and review process described here, it is quite probable that a company may not find a tool

TABLE 4.4

Agile versus Traditional Project Management Tools Utilization

Traditional PM Software Tool Activity	Agile PM Software Tool Activity
Schedule activities	Product backlog maintenance
Manage activity dependencies	Create release and iteration plans
Address potential risks	Burndown/Burnup Charts
Schedule tasks	Task boards
Critical path(s)	

that is desired. This would mean that the company would merely have to pick a tool that is best suited in comparison to others and move forward or decide upon other options such as using traditional project management tools to manage the agile project such as MS Project or MS Excel. Agile tools include JIRA, Rally, and Version One. Table 4.4 shows which types of project management tasks are used with agile and which ones are used for traditional project management.

Agile Automated Tools

Automated tools are used in agile environments for the purposes of conducting test-driven development (TDD) or acceptance test-driven development (ATDD).[*] Recall from Chapter 3 that TDD is an Extreme Programming (XP) practice where the developers write tests before developing the code. TDD is designed to shorten the process in order to obtain early feedback. Tests are written as unit tests using automated tools such as NUnit or JUnit before the actual code is written. On the first run of the tests, failure will occur because the code does not exist as of yet. The code writing process begins and continues until the tests pass. In the event that additional functionality needs to be added to a particular portion of the code, this process is repeated. Shortly thereafter, the code is refactored for efficiency and development is complete for that particular component of functionality.

Why are tests run prior to the development of the code? With traditional software project management, just the opposite occurs. The code is written and then testing is done. There are several reasons for writing tests prior to code development:

---

[*] Griffiths, M. (2012).

- The agile framework specifies that test-driven development puts more emphasis on understanding how the functionality will work for the end user. This way of thinking about the outcome prior to implementation has been shown to lead to much better designs and greater product success from the end client's perspective.
- Testing is less costly early in the process as opposed to later. This leads to lower overall costs for the project.
- Writing tests first is a good practice that has been shown to lead to better overall test coverage.

With ATDD, the focus is on user stories. These types of tests are designed to support acceptance by the customer or end users. These tests are functional in nature and are designed to demonstrate that specific product features work as intended. If the customer is satisfied, then the component that is tied to the user story is labeled as "done" and it is considered to be formally accepted.

Build Automation Tools

Build tools are used on many types of projects and the agile framework is no exception. These tools are used for automating the process that compiles computer source code into machine language binary code. Build automation is being discussed because it is the focal point of continuous integration of the code on agile projects. Continuous integration is a software development practice. The development team regularly integrates new and modified code into a repository for the product. Build automation tools use a built-in scripting language to compile computer source code, create release notes, and deploy code to test, staging, and development environments. Developers are typically the users of these types of tools because they handle the code and related activities. These tools are designed to eliminate build errors and lessen the time it takes to get a software build out to a particular environment.

In addition to the automated testing tool types identified in the preceding paragraphs, graphical user interface (GUI) testing may occur on the agile project for regression testing, just as with traditional project management software development. These tests can be run back to back to demonstrate an overall system test to ensure that changes to parts of the code did not inadvertently "break" other product features.

Cameras

Why would we need a camera on an agile project? Well, why not? The author has seen a camera used on non-agile projects to take pictures of whiteboards. As a matter of fact, this is the same reason that we would use cameras on the agile project: to capture important whiteboard information. After capture, this information can be sent to others, posted to the team's collaboration site, or developed into a formal documentation source.

Collaboration Tools

Collaboration tools are used on agile projects to allow the team to share information. What does a collaboration tool do? It provides the means for a team or stakeholders to collaborate. This is very important on the agile project because the team needs to have a multitude of discussions with regard to the delivery of the product. In addition, agile project team members engage in "games" that are designed to achieve a shared understanding of complicated or unclear project issues so that a team consensus can be obtained.

It was previously mentioned that the agile team size is typically six to ten members. There are many exceptions to this team size. On occasion, agile projects cannot support colocation and this results in distributed teams with their own set of challenges. Face-to-face interactions are recommended for the agile team, however, collaborative technology enables other types of communication to work just as well. In the case where some of the agile team is not in the same physical location, there are other options such as:

- Instant messenger (IM)
- Interactive whiteboards
- Web-enabled meetings
- Conference calls

There are additional options for collaboration as well, regardless of which type of tool is selected. The idea is to provide consistent feedback and to keep all stakeholders engaged.

Task Boards

The task board is a commonly used tool on agile projects.[*] It is often the focus point for the daily standup meeting and it serves as a central source of information that is applicable to the entire team. The task board is simple to use and does not prohibit the display of any type of information that is relevant to the team's progress.

CHAPTER SUMMARY

It is not uncommon to hear that many companies experience difficulty in selecting the appropriate tools to use in their agile environments. User friendliness appears to be one of the leading factors when searching for the most appropriate tool. It is not clear whether companies are satisfied or dissatisfied with their agile tool choices. It is clear, however, that many companies have embraced the agile framework and many others have plans to do the same.

---

[*] Griffiths (2012), Agile Alliance (2014).

5

Agile Stakeholder Engagement

This chapter discusses the importance of stakeholder engagement on the agile project. This is an essential practice that ensures a successful product delivery. We concentrate on important concepts such as:

- Getting the right stakeholders for the project
- Cementing stakeholder involvement
- Managing the interests of stakeholders

The uniqueness of the agile project requires that stakeholders participate in demonstrations that show progress and product capabilities. This practice keeps the stakeholder engagement levels very high. In addition, stakeholders remain informed about the project status on a regular basis. In order to avoid surprises and unacceptable products, frequent discussions of what "done" looks like need to occur. In addition, discussions with regard to estimations and projections should occur so that stakeholders can make decisions from unbiased information.

TRADITIONAL STAKEHOLDER MANAGEMENT

The fifth edition of *A Guide to the Project Management Body of Knowledge (PMBOK® Guide)*[*] has only recently included project stakeholder management as a separate knowledge area within the traditional project management framework. This change was incorporated into the *PMBOK® Guide* in 2013. It is well known in the IT industry that proper stakeholder management is a critical element of successful project management.

---

[*] PMI. (2013).

There are some who may wonder why the PMI made the decision to add project stakeholder management as an additional knowledge area in the *PMBOK® Guide*. According to the PMI, one reason for this particular change was to associate a higher level of importance to stakeholder management. Its prior inclusion under project communications management could have possibly made this knowledge area seem unintentionally insignificant. This change made by PMI has unquestionably put additional focus on project stakeholder management and illuminates its proper level of significance in the attainment of project success.

We now discuss traditional project management and make the appropriate comparisons to agile concepts. This is being done so that readers can better understand the differences during the application of either type of method. The PMI's stakeholder management knowledge area has been expanded to include four distinct processes as identified below.

1. *Identify Stakeholders:* The process is used to identify the people, groups, or entities that could have an impact, could be affected, or are affected by the project that is being undertaken (including being affected by a project decision, outcome, or activity). This identification process would also include a documented acknowledgment of the stakeholders' involvement, influence, and their power on the success of the project.
2. *Develop Stakeholder Management Plan:* This process develops the management level strategy to engage stakeholders appropriately throughout the project. This process includes an analysis of the stakeholders based on their needs and interest levels, and their potential impact on the success of the project.
3. *Manage Stakeholder Engagement:* This is the process of communicating and interacting with stakeholders in order to meet their expectations and needs so that adequate stakeholder engagement can be obtained throughout the project.
4. *Control Stakeholder Engagement:* This is the process of monitoring stakeholders and their project interactions so that the engagement strategy can be adjusted if needed.

Now that we have provided an overview of the rather newly created traditional project management stakeholder management knowledge area, we discuss agile stakeholder management. Once again, it is important that we engage project stakeholders because it is a requirement for the attainment of project success regardless of what type of project is being undertaken.

AGILE STAKEHOLDER MANAGEMENT CONCEPTS[*]

We have established the importance of engaging stakeholders on projects in order to increase the likelihood of success; it is equally important to understand the need for the "right" stakeholders. This means there is a need for stakeholders who can make decisions so that the momentum can be maintained on the project.

The Right People

Agile projects must be able to maintain a sustainable pace so that when decisions have to be made there won't be any unnecessary delays. This is where the right stakeholders come into play. The agile stakeholder needs to be available, engaged, and able to contribute toward moving the project forward in the right direction when needed. Lengthy decision making, bureaucratic delays, or unmovable obstacles do not align very well in the agile realm. In situations such as these, the agile project manager should have more than one stakeholder who is willing and ready to make difficult decisions in a timely fashion. In many cases, the Product Owner or customer can take on the role of dealing with bureaucracy.

Stakeholder Management

How are stakeholders' interests managed on the agile project? Who has the responsibility for managing stakeholders' interests? We start with the easy question first. The Product Owner is likely the individual responsible for the actual management of the stakeholders on the agile project. In other cases, the agile project manager takes on this responsibility.

An excellent way to manage stakeholders on the agile project is to ensure that everyone is fully versed in agile principles, practices, and project methodologies. This may involve training or some informal way of ensuring that the benefits of agile project management are understood.

---

[*] Griffiths, M. (2012).

A ScrumMaster or agile coach is the perfect role to communicate these benefits to the team on a regular basis. Lack of understanding as to how the agile project is supposed to work can result in stakeholders feeling excluded or frustrated. Once a common understanding of agility is achieved and the foundation is established, fears and concerns should lessen. This stakeholder management milestone is expected to result in the interested parties becoming more engaged on the project.

A larger stakeholder management task that should be undertaken is addressing the concerns of the stakeholder groups. The fact that project decisions have the potential to affect individuals and groups requires that stakeholders be provided with the necessary information related to their particular interests. It is the hope of all stakeholders that the project that is being undertaken will affect their interests in a positive way. It is possible, however, that the project can affect some stakeholders in a negative fashion. In either case, stakeholders want to know the project's impact on their interests. The concerns of those potentially affected need to be addressed so that all stakeholder groups understand their position with regard to the project's results or decisions. Only through stakeholder engagement and management can the concerns of the groups be addressed.

Stakeholders are inclusive of customers, users, and the sponsor. This group of individuals regularly interacts with the Product Owner, development team, and agile leader to assist with the creation of the product. Recall that the customer is a person or an entire organization that procures the product, service, or result that is being created by the project. When agile is first introduced into an organization, it is important to align stakeholders' understanding of agile methods with the project's requirements. This should be done in order to overcome any potential knowledge gaps that might occur. Stakeholder values should be incorporated into the project's priorities and implementation. This really boils down to synching the project's priorities with stakeholders' priorities. An agile project should never engage in work that is not valued or supported by project stakeholders. We have discussed stakeholder groups and now clarify the types of groups that are typically found on agile projects. Table 5.1 represents a listing of the possible concerns that the groups may have.

Vendor Management

External stakeholders who provide products or services may potentially need agile education. If at all possible, agile vendors should be selected

TABLE 5.1

Stakeholder Groups and Types of Concerns

Stakeholder Group	Concerns
Users	Product features, value
Sponsors	Costs, schedule, risks
Agile project team	Agile methods uncertainty
Corporate officials	Change
Product owner	Gaining support
Vendors	Contracts

on agile projects. Vendors are evaluated based on how well they satisfy the contractual terms that have been agreed upon. Requirements on the agile project are expected to change rather frequently and, as a result, agile contracts have been created in response to this need. Chapter 14 covers agile contracts in greater detail. It is highly probable that vendors may require agile education prior to working in an agile environment. A cost–benefit analysis should be conducted in order to determine which vendors might require training. Any type of agile education provided should include agile values, practices, goals, and related benefits. This ensures that stakeholders are fully aware of why the project is being implemented with agile methods.

Ensuring Stakeholder Engagement

Stakeholders must remain engaged and committed throughout the entire project. Stakeholder involvement should be monitored so that there is proper visibility into the levels of engagement that are required. It should be understood that the customer, sponsor, and users of the product are the most important stakeholders on the agile project. We base this ranking on the agile principle that states: *"Our highest priority is to satisfy the customer through early and continuous delivery of valuable software."*

It is important to understand that stakeholders may need incentives to remain faithfully engaged. Many stakeholders are extremely busy with additional projects and responsibilities. Recognizing the efforts and contributions of stakeholders is a sure way to keep involvement levels strong. Praise and admiration appeal to most and these techniques should be utilized as ways of showing appreciation.

Another way to keep stakeholders involved is to demonstrate a working product as a success factor. The agile principle, *"Working software is the primary measure of progress,"* implies that the demonstration of working software is a measure of how much progress has been made. Stakeholders should be included in these working software demonstrations as a way to keep them involved. Progress is good for the morale of all stakeholders and it also shows that value is being delivered on a consistent basis.

Yet another way to keep stakeholders engaged is to involve them in the grooming and prioritization of the product's backlog. The end result of this is that stakeholders are aware of what is going into the product and they have a voice as to the value that goes into the product. For full engagement of stakeholders, it is probably a good idea to include them in all of the project's meetings so that there won't be any surprises or situations where they are caught off guard or feel as if what they value has not been considered. During meetings, different stakeholder groups can be managed with a time-boxed approach. For example, if a meeting is 30 minutes in duration, agile methods require that the meeting is stopped at the end of the time-boxed period. This is a way to keep order and avoid chaos during meetings. Readers need to be mindful that it is very possible that some stakeholders may present themselves as "problems" and may actually be a hindrance to the project. This is where the ScrumMaster or agile project manager should exercise soft skills in order to understand the rationale behind these difficulties and determine a positive way to deal with these types of stakeholders. Stakeholder management requires the establishment of a process for the escalation of issues that warrant a higher level of authority to resolve. The agile project must remain obstacle free in order to reach its goals.

STAKEHOLDER TOOLS AND TECHNIQUES

Stakeholders must all have a similar level of understanding with regard to the project requirements. Miscommunication or misunderstandings need to be corrected as quickly as possible as there is no time to waste. The agile project is fast paced and progress must be realized rather rapidly. What this boils down to is the need for tools and technology to keep everyone moving in the right direction. We discuss several tools and techniques that can be used to support the attainment of a common understanding for all stakeholders.

Agile Modeling

Stakeholders need to be a part of agile modeling because of the meaningful discussions that take place during these sessions. Whiteboards are often used to display design models and provide the means for discussion of project issues, problems, and concerns. Use cases, data models, and screen mockups are created during agile software modeling events. The purpose of modeling is to assist with delivering value to the product and stakeholder input is extremely important to this process.

Personas

In order to align stakeholders' understanding of the project so that there are no gaps between what the customer asks for and to ensure that the development team understands what has been asked for, a persona can be used as a tool to uncover mismatches. This tool can be very useful in gaining consensus among stakeholders.

Simply put, a *persona* is a role that is taken on by an actor. Most of us are familiar with the term "actor." The unified modeling language (UML) uses actors (i.e., a user or another system) to describe how users operate a system. The persona has a similar meaning and purpose. The persona is used to help stakeholders understand and clarify the characteristics of the users of the end product.

Website Wireframe

A website wireframe is a fancy term describing a technique used to define product functionality. These tools are used as a way to ensure that everyone has the same understanding of how the product will work. It must be made clear that wireframes are not used to show what the product will look like. Developers can use this type of tool to create a product prototype and obtain feedback. In any event, the purpose of wireframes is merely to gain clarification of what "done" means to the project team or to verify a particular technical approach. Although the name "wireframe" may sound complex, developers can use Microsoft PowerPoint and Visio to create these items. Simply put, wireframes have been referred to in the past as technical diagrams. The wireframe is a visual tool that stakeholders can adjust and use to gain consensus on a product mockup. Team plans can also be validated with wireframes.

User Stories

User stories have the same meaning as requirements. This is just another term to describe the desired capabilities of the product. User stories represent the means to gain a common understanding of functionality among the stakeholders. In 2003, Bill Wake[*] originated the criteria that define the attributes of an effective user story as identified with the acronym INVEST:

(I) Independent: User stories should not be designed to be dependent upon another user story.

(N) Negotiable: User stories should be negotiable in terms of functionality and associated costs.

(V) Valuable: User stories should always be associated with business value.

(E) Estimatable: User stories should always be "estimatable" in terms of the time it takes to develop and the amount of costs involved.

(S) Small: User stories should be small and easy to estimate within a time frame of between one half-day to a maximum of 10 days.

(T) Testable: As with most requirements, user stories should always be testable.

Stakeholder Communications Management

According to the PMI (2013), project communications management is inclusive of all processes that ensure the timely and applicable planning, collection, creation, distribution, storage, retrieval, management, control, monitoring, and disposition of project information. For the agile project, and in contrast to traditional project management, the preferred method of communication is mainly face to face because this method has the capability of transferring the greatest amount of information in any given period of time. Feedback can be obtained almost instantaneously when communicating face to face. The fastest way is the best way for the agile project, however, we know that the agile project requires transparency and information needs to be displayed.

---

[*] Agile Alliance. (2014).

Information Displays

Agile project data need to be visible to the agile team and stakeholders at all times. We have previously discussed whiteboards during our discussion of Scrum and we now summarize this information for agile project management as a whole. The agile project needs visibility and display of the following types of information:

- Current iteration product features: The list of product features for the current iteration.
- Remaining product features: The remaining product features to be completed for the current iteration.
- Team velocity information: The amount of work that the development team can complete for an iteration.
- Defects: Discrepancies or errors that have been identified.
- Retrospective information: Lessons learned from the iteration.
- Risks: A list of uncertainties that have been uncovered.
- Burndown/Burnup Charts: These two charts show progress and determine when the project or a release should be completed. Burndown charts show the work that remains; Burnup Charts show what has been delivered.

CHAPTER SUMMARY

This concludes our discussion on the main focus areas regarding agile stakeholder management. Following is a summary of the important concepts discussed in this chapter:

- Face-to-face communication is the preferred way to communicate on the agile project.
- Velocity defines the work capacity of the team.
- Stakeholders must be engaged throughout the project in order to ensure a successful outcome.
- Stakeholders must be managed and their needs addressed.
- Agile contracts are different from those used in traditional project management.

- Stakeholder engagement activities should be visible.
- Project information should be visible to support transparency.

It is very important that stakeholders are engaged on the agile project. This will ensure that the agile team builds exactly what the customer expects. Stakeholder engagement is the way to ensure that the delivered product is of high quality and meets or exceeds expectations.

6

Agile Documentation?

This chapter focuses on the documentation requirements or lack thereof on agile projects. The question mark behind the chapter's title is not a discrepancy. It represents the question that is addressed throughout this discussion. As an overview of what is to come throughout this chapter, the answer will not be "Yes" or "No" but more of a "How much?" We recall the agile value: "*Working software over comprehensive documentation.*" Agile methods value working software more than comprehensive documentation, however, this does not necessarily mean there is no value in capturing information in written form on the project.

AGILE DOCUMENTATION BEST PRACTICES

Some agile experts believe that documentation actually increases project risk.[*] They feel that if documentation must be developed, the motive should be for efficiency purposes only. Agile project documentation should only be developed, according to some experts, for the attainment of specific goals. We begin our discussion with an overview of agile documentation best practices.

Selecting What to Document

Documentation requirements on a traditional project require that specifications be documented (i.e., requirements or design specs). In contrast, the agile project uses what are referred to as *specifications in executable*

---

[*] Ambler, S. 2012a. Ambler, S. 2012b.

Test Driven Development (TDD) Process

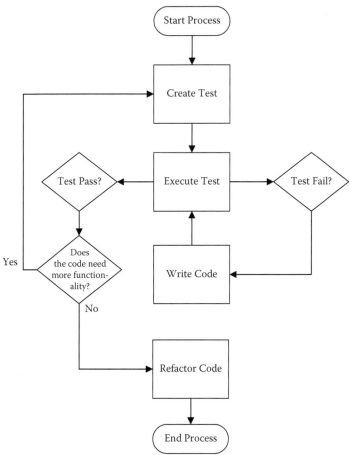

FIGURE 6.1

The test-driven development process.

forms such as, for example, a test created for a test-driven development (TDD) scenario. TDD is a software-based technique that requires tests to be written prior to the creation of the code. A TDD cycle has several steps as shown in Figure 6.1. Code created during this activity is considered to be a *dynamic specification* used to validate a user story's functionality. This agile documentation concept is referred to as "single source information." It won't be necessary to create static documentation in a case like this because TDD is very dynamic in nature. In addition, the preference is always to use an executable specification rather than a written one.

Stable Information

Documentation should be delayed until the latest possible time on the agile project. This is referred to as *"document late,"* an agile documentation best practice. In the case of critical material, the recommendation is to take notes for later use. Formal documentation should be developed toward the project's end. Hypothetical information should not be selected for documentation. With regard to system documentation, it would be ideal to use built-in software tools to generate this type of information.

Simple Documentation

Agile experts believe that comprehensive documentation is not a method that guarantees a successful project and that too much documentation on the agile project can contribute to project failure. When documentation is created, it should be concise and simple. Short documents are considered to be more trustworthy than those that are longer. Why would this be the case? We would not expect the shorter document to contain information in detail, however, it would be relatively easy to use short documents as a map to point us to other documents that contain more information. There is more trust in a short document because we can easily determine its level of accuracy as opposed to a large document that has the potential to have a larger number of errors. Lastly, information should never be repeated in multiple places and it is acceptable to use references rather than the actual information within agile documentation.

Minimal Document Overlap

Information should be in one place only and overlapping should not occur. In the event that an overlap does occur, it should be very minimal. Documents should be just good enough to satisfy a project goal. One-page topics is a good practice and using small documents as the foundation to create larger ones is recommended.

Proper Place for Documents

The proper place for documentation should always be based on the needs of the customer and the customer's choice of location. According to the

Quality Work Principle,[*] information should be recorded in the place where it will enhance the work. This principle states that: "Nobody likes sloppy work. The people doing the work don't like it because it's something they can't be proud of, the people coming along later to refactor the work (for whatever reason) don't like it because it's harder to understand and to update, and the end users won't like the work because it's likely fragile and/or doesn't meet their expectations."

Publicly Displayed Information

When information is displayed publicly by means of a whiteboard or a website, this is referred to as using an *information radiator*. The better the communication is on the project, the less the project will need extensive documentation. This is the reason why people and their interactions are valued more than comprehensive documentation. Agile methods believe that face to face is a more effective way to communicate in comparison with lengthy documentation. Figure 6.2 shows the effectiveness of several types of communications channels from the agile perspective.

Create Documentation with a Purpose

Documentation should only be developed in situations where an objective needs to be reached for the project as a whole. This requisite should be clear, essential, and immediate. In contrast to traditional project management, agile methods never dictate the adherence to a repeatable process that uses templates. In order to be effective, there should never be an expectation that one size will fit all when it comes to agile documentation. Agile methods are adaptive based on the needs of the project and most documentation should never be created unless requested by a stakeholder.

Focus on Customer Needs

It is best to communicate with the document's audience so that an understanding of the requirements is established. This would mean that the customer who requested the documentation would need to be involved. Negotiations with the customer may need to take place so that only the

---

[*] Ambler, S. (2012b).

Methods of Communication

FIGURE 6.2
Methods of communications. (Derived from Ambler, S. (2012). *Agile Modeling: Best Practices for Agile/Lean Documentation*. Retrieved from http://www.agilemodeling.com/ essays/agileDocumentationBestPractices.htm. With permission.)

minimum requirements can be provided. Questions that need to be asked might be the following:

1. What does this customer do?
2. How does this customer do what they do?
3. How does this customer want to use the documentation that is being requested?

This would be considered an exercise in determining the needs of the customer and providing what is needed and nothing more.

Let the Customer Determine Document Value

The agile project must always deliver value to the customer and providing documentation is no exception to this rule. The author of any customer documentation must provide value and it would then be the customer's responsibility to verify that the value provided is of an acceptable level. In addition to value added, it must also be determined that the document has real meaning.

Iterative Documentation

Just as the product is delivered iteratively, documentation should be delivered in this manner as well. The recommended way to create documentation is to write a draft, gain feedback, and then update the document based on the feedback that has been provided. The iterative approach ensures that the intended audience provides the necessary feedback so that their needs are satisfied. Feedback also provides information from the stakeholder as to the amount of value added.

Better Ways to Communicate

We previously mentioned Figure 6.2 (Methods of Communication) as showing that paper-based communication has the lowest ranking for effectiveness. A major problem with communications is the understanding of the information presented and not necessarily the actual documentation. The project's goal is not to bury or overburden users with documentation, but to ensure that the developed product has high value and performs as intended. Documentation does have its usefulness in terms of improving the transfer of knowledge. Face-to-face conversations have the highest level of effectiveness on the agile project. Documentation is good for situations where there is distance between team members. Recall that the agile team is colocated so there is very little need for documentation as a result of this physical configuration.

Current Documents

Update-to-date modeling documents are more valuable than those that have not been kept current. It is a positive indication when these documents are current because it is certain that value has been added. These types of documents should be used as starting points when developing new material.

When to Update Documents

Model diagrams (design, interface, etc.) should only be updated when it is absolutely necessary. This means that updates should only take place when there is pain associated with not having the model updated, or in other words, there is a negative impact. The logic behind this method is based on the fact that code does in fact change frequently, however, models should only be good enough, and very little time should be spent updating documentation. If the model is good enough, then that would be acceptable because agile methods don't require perfection in documentation. Just good enough is enough.

Documentation Requirements

Agile methods view documentation requests as requirements. This means that documentation requests should be estimated, given a priority, and treated as a task. When treating documentation as a requirement, the customer should consider this action as a business decision. Documents should only be developed as a result of a stakeholder's request.

Require Justification for Documentation

Prior to creating documents, a best practice is to make sure that the requester fully understands what is being asked. It is a good idea to gain an understanding of why the document is needed. The requester must also be made aware that documentation is not "free" and that there will be associated costs involved. Often when questions are asked, it is revealed that the need for the document is not genuine. There must be a benefit in developing the document that must be larger than the cost of creation and maintenance. The need for the documentation should exist rather than just the desire to have it. A stakeholder must make the decision to invest in the creation of the document. In addition, the documentation must be created to provide the best value and the request should never be taken lightly.

Required Documentation

There is some documentation that may be actually required. In this case, the requirements are to "minimally" develop only what is absolutely necessary. On occasion, user manuals, product support, or operations documentation may be required. It is important to remember that the main focus of the project is to develop and deliver the software product. Making sure that the product can be maintained, supported, and operated is important as well. In most cases, only high-level information should be documented and details should be kept at a minimum.

Writing Experience Required

When feasible, a technical writer should be utilized to create project documentation. These individuals have experience in organizing and presenting information. In the event that a writing professional is not an option, the ownership of a document can be shared so that several people can contribute. Other options include dictation software that generates the words as they are spoken, enrolling in a technical writing course, and writing with a partner, which is referred to as "pair documenting."

CHAPTER SUMMARY

We now provide a summary of the important concepts covered on agile documentation.

- Agile documents should be kept simple.
- Agile documents should be "just good enough."
- Agile document requests should require justification.
- Documents should be updated only when necessary or when there will be "pain" if not updated.
- Most documentation should only be done when requested by a stakeholder and justified.
- Documentation is the least effective way to communicate on the agile project.
- Document creation should be done iteratively.
- Documents should have minimal overlap.
- Documentation should always add value.
- Working software is valued more than documentation.

7

Agile Tracking and Reporting

This chapter discusses tracking and reporting requirements in the agile environment.[*] At the end of the iterations, certain information is of particular interest to stakeholders. A review of several of these items follows.

- *Product Backlog:* The backlog includes all product requirements. These user stories are selected for development based on the priority levels assigned by the customer. High-priority items are developed first and those that have a low priority may be postponed for later iterations.
- *Iteration Backlog (e.g., Sprint Backlog):* These items include the list of user stories that the developers have agreed to complete for a particular iteration. The items in the iteration backlog cannot be changed once the iteration has begun.

We have identified some of the information that stakeholders have interest in and now we need to determine how these data points should best be presented. In the agile environment, a best practice is to use a task board that visually displays relevant project information. A task board helps with the delivery of value on the agile project. It offers benefits such as the perceived improvement of the project data accuracy and removal of roadblocks to stakeholder interactions. The reader should remember that agile is about simplicity. The task board is a simple tool that supports increased visibility on the agile project. The task board can be used to display information for the (1) overall project, (2) a release, or (3) the current iteration. In addition, the author believes that the number of defects can be reported on a task board. Information is typically displayed in three columns: to do, in progress, and done. User stories are displayed in each column with their assigned story points (See Figure 7.1 for details).

---

[*] Agile Alliance. (2014).

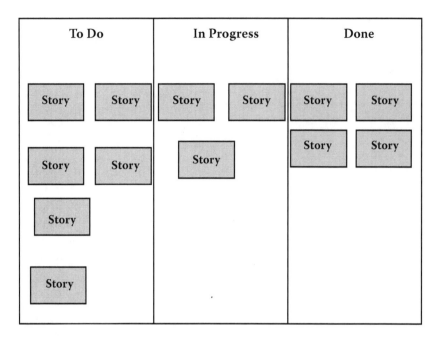

FIGURE 7.1
Agile task board.

Additional information that is reported in the agile environment includes but is not limited to the following:

- *Burndown Chart:* This particular chart is used to show when the project is expected to be completed. The level of effort that is remaining on the project can be shown in terms of story points or hours. Recall from Chapter 3, Figure 3.2, the Burndown Chart example.
- *Team Velocity:* The development team's velocity is denoted by a number that indicates how many user stories they can develop into functionality during the iterations. Velocity is recorded for all iterations and this determines when a project is expected to be completed. For example, if a team has an average of 40 story points per iteration, the product backlog has 400 story points remaining; then we divide 400/40 and we get 10. This means that in 10 additional iterations, the project is expected to be completed.* See Figure 7.2 for an illustration of team velocity information. The data can be graphed and visually displayed using MS Excel.

---

* Griffiths, M. (2012).

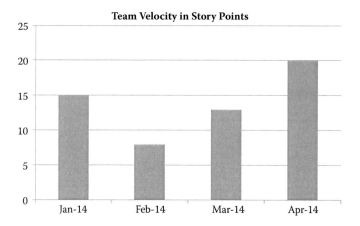

FIGURE 7.2
Team velocity example.

The example above shows the team's velocity on a monthly basis. Another option is to show the team's velocity on an iteration basis. When tracking team velocity over several iterations, this information can be used to determine when the actual project is forecast to be completed. During the early iterations, it is expected that team velocity will vary and then become consistent later in the project. This is normal because of the newness of the environment to the agile team.

EARNED VALUE ON AGILE PROJECTS

Story points are a good measurement of the volume of work planned and completed. This information can be used for calculating earned value. According to the PMI (2013), earned value management (EVM)[*] is a method that uses scope, schedule, and resources to evaluate project performance and progress. We have provided an overview of EVM formulas and definitions below:

Planned Value (PV): The approved budget for the scheduled work.
Earned Value (EV): The measure of the work performed based on the approved budget.

---

[*] PMI. (2013).

Actual Cost (AC): The actual costs incurred for the work that has been performed on an activity during an explicit time period.

Schedule Variance (SV): A measure of the schedule performance calculated as the difference between the earned value and the planned value. Formula: $SV = EV - PV$

Interpretation of results:

Positive = Ahead of schedule (good)

Neutral (0) = On schedule (okay)

Negative = Behind schedule (not good)

Cost Variance (CV): The amount of budget shortfall or leftover at a specific point in time calculated as the difference between earned value and the actual cost. Formula: $CV = EV - AC$

Interpretation of results:

Positive = Under planned costs (good)

Neutral (0) = At planned costs (okay)

Negative = Over planned costs (not good)

Schedule Performance Index (SPI): A measure of the schedule efficiency calculated as the ratio of earned value to planned value. Formula: $SPI = EV/PV$

Interpretation of results:

>1.0 = Ahead of schedule (good)

Exactly 1.0 = On schedule (okay)

Less than 1.0 = Behind schedule (not good)

Cost Performance Index (CPI): A measure of the cost efficiency of the budgeted resources calculated as a ratio of earned value to actual cost. Formula: $CPI = EV/AC$

Interpretation of results:

>1.0 = Under planned costs (good)

Exactly 1.0 = At planned costs (okay)

<1.0 = Over planned costs (not good)

In order to calculate earned value on the agile project, we would need to consider the following:

- The number of story points for a release, an iteration, or the prioritized product backlog for the project. This number is used to measure the amount of planned work. This will be the foundation for all of the earned value calculations.
- The number of planned iterations.
  - 15

- The number of story points planned in the backlog.
  - 100
- The budget planned for the entire backlog.
  - $100,000
- The start date of the project.
  - This date is 01/13/2014 and each iteration is 2 weeks long.
  - Current date is 04/01/2014; 12 weeks have passed; 6 iterations completed.
- The number of iterations that have been completed.
  - This is a measurement of the expected percent complete (EPC) calculated by dividing the number of iterations completed by the total number of planned iterations.
  - Sample data: 6 iterations completed/15 total planned iterations
  - Expected percent complete = 6/15 = 40%

We calculate the schedule performance index (SPI) for a fictitious project.

- SPI = Completed story points/planned story points
- For example, Completed story points = 60 and planned story points = 60
- Velocity = 10 story points per iteration (10 × 6 = 60); Recall that 6 iterations have been completed and velocity is 10 per iteration.
- SPI = 60/60
- SPI = 1.0 (on schedule)

Calculate the cost performance index (CPI):

- CPI = EV/AC
- Let's say the 60 story points were budgeted at $60,000 and actual costs are $75,000.
- CPI = $60,000/75,000
- CPI =.80 (Over the planned costs)

Calculate the schedule variance (SV):

- SV = EV – PV
- Let's say the EV = $60,000 from our example above.
- PV = $60,000
- SV = $60,000 – $60,000
- SV = $0 (on schedule)

Calculate the cost variance (CV):

- CV = EV – AC
- Let's say the EV = $60,000.
- AC = $75,000
- CV = $60,000 – $75,000
- CV = -$15,000 (over the planned cost by this amount)

It must be clear that EVM has its place on the agile project. We should be cautious with the interpretation of the results, however. The project may be on track in terms of schedule, costs, and scope, but the main objective on the agile project is to deliver value to the customer. What we actually need to track and report on is value. Earned value is not the same as business value. We must never lose our focus on delivering business value for the customer! To further clarify, earned value is a measure of work that has been completed whereas business value (discussed in Chapter 1) describes the well-being of a business. This includes economic profits and other forms of tangible and intangible value including but not limited to employee or customer value.

CUMULATIVE FLOW DIAGRAMS

Another type of graph that is used on the agile project is known as a cumulative flow diagram. This is a graphical representation of the total number of features that have been completed and are in progress based on a particular time frame. Figure 7.3 shows a sample diagram. Note that these graphs can be generated in MS Excel.

WORK IN PROGRESS (WIP)

Work in progress refers to work that has not yet been completed. Kanban development is based upon the Lean production system that is used at Toyota Motor Company. The word *Kanban* means "signboard" in Japanese, another word for task board. Kanban development, a Lean/agile method, limits work that is in progress so that issues can be identified, waste can be

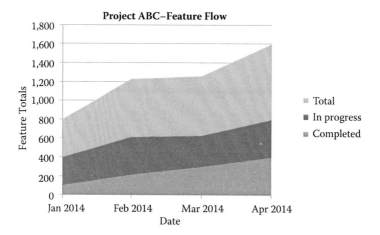

FIGURE 7.3
Cumulative flow diagram.

minimized,* and costs that are related to changes can be limited. In addition to WIP, Kanban uses the "pull system" (based on actual or consumed demand) rather than the "push system" (based on forecast demand).† With the task board, value is visually displayed and the team has easy access to the information. With Kanban, teams are invigorated to try different methods and tactics. This results in continuous improvement under the pull system. The end result is that waste is eliminated or reduced.

CHAPTER SUMMARY

This concludes our discussion on tracking and reporting value. Some of our metrics such as earned value are used in a similar way as in traditional project management. For the agile project, we are concerned about tracking and reporting of value delivered to the customer. It is very important to track and report value in the agile environment. We need to ensure that the project will be completed as planned, value is being delivered to the client, and the project's status is reported to the stakeholders in a timely fashion. The tools and techniques described in this chapter represent the means by which we can accomplish the agile project's tracking and reporting goals.

---

* Kanban development is based on the Lean production system that is used at Toyota.
† Consumers pull and suppliers push.

8

Agile Project Management Process

Although there is some variation in many of the agile methods, there are overall activities common to all of them. Figure 8.1 illustrates the entire framework of the agile project management process at a high level. One can expect to see all, if not most, of the processes in the different agile methods. We now provide a detailed overview of the processes within the agile project management framework. We start with a discussion of the agile project feasibility study which is the initial stage in the agile project management process. A discussion follows as outlined in the diagram.

AGILE PROJECT MANAGEMENT

In order to put the agile project management process into the proper perspective for our readers, we have provided a summary of the differences between agile methods and traditional project management as outlined in Table 8.1.

PROJECT FEASIBILITY

The best way to determine if a project is feasible is to conduct the proper assessment prior to the project start. The project under review for selection needs to be worthwhile and there needs to be adequate justification for the project in terms of what it will bring to the business in terms of value. The agile project with its value-driven approach will display results early

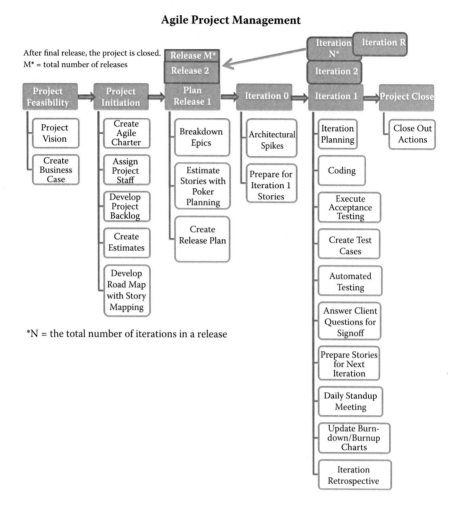

Agile Project Management

FIGURE 8.1
Agile Project Management Process.

and this in turn proves the worth of the project to the stakeholders.* The project feasibility process has two activities and a discussion follows:

1. Create business case.
2. Project vision.

Create Business Case

Business case development is usually organization specific and the intent is to justify why a particular project must be undertaken based on the

---

* SCRUMstudy. (2013).

TABLE 8.1

Summary of Differences between Agile and Traditional Project Management

	Agile Methods	Traditional Project Management
Focus is on	People	Processes
Documentation Level	Low, only as required	High
Process Style	Iterative and incremental	Linear
Initial Planning Requirements	Low	High
Requirements Prioritization	Based upon business value and regularly updated	Fixed within the project plan
Quality	Customer focused	Process focused
Organization Style	Self-organized	Managed
Management Style	Decentralized	Centralized
Changes	Backlog updated	Formal change management in place
Leadership Style	Collaborative; servant leadership	Command and control
Performance Measurement	Business value	Conformity to the project plan
Return on Investment (ROI)	Early and throughout the project life	End of the project life
Customer Involvement level	High and throughout the project	Involvement level is varied and depends upon the project life cycle

Source: SCRUMstudy, 2013.

needs of the business. A business case for an agile project is similar to one that is developed for a traditional project; the difference will be the light documentation and the heavy focus on early business value, which is not very common for the traditional project. *

Project Vision

The project vision is a simple statement that represents the goal for the agile project. It is the responsibility of the Product Owner to create the project vision along with input from the agile team. A vision statement should be established that describes what the project should achieve, why the project is being undertaken, and what the definition is for project success.

---

* Griffiths, M. (2012).

AGILE PROJECT INITIATION

As illustrated in Figure 8.1, project initiation is the second step in the agile project management process. According to the *PMBOK® Guide* (2013), project initiation is the set of activities necessary to define a new project (or phase) and obtain the authorization to begin the project (or phase).[*] Project initiation has the same intent on all projects; however, the activities are somewhat different between agile project management and traditional project management. The initiation process for agile projects includes the following activities:

1. Create agile charter.
2. Assign the project staff.
3. Develop project backlog.
4. Create estimates.
5. Develop road map with story mapping.

A discussion of each activity follows.

Create Agile Charter

The process for creating the project charter on an agile project is similar to the PMI's traditional project management process: develop project charter.[†] According to the *PMBOK® Guide* (2013), this process develops the document that officially authorizes the project to start and gives the project manager the authority to use resources. With regard to agile project management, creating the agile charter requires the creation of a very flexible document that allows the team to respond quickly to changes. There are, of course, differences between a traditional project management charter and an agile charter. For the agile project, the project charter outlines the project objectives and expected outcomes of the project. Instead of authorizing just the project manager as in traditional project management, the agile project charter authorizes the entire team to start the project.[‡] Other differences between the traditional and agile charters may include the following:

---

[*] PMI. (2013).
[†] PMI. (2013).
[‡] SCRUMstudy. (2013).

- There is very little detail in the agile charter.
- The charter needs to specify the agile method so that everyone is on the same page. This applies in the case where there is a change in the agile method or agility is new to the organization.
- Agile charters are smaller than traditional project management charters.
- The agile charter has to allow for changes throughout the project.
- The agile charter answers the Five Ws and the One H questions (who, what, why, when, where, and how).

The Five Ws and the One H questions were written by Rudyard Kipling, a novelist, writer, and poet who was born in Bombay in 1865 and died in 1936. The poem is titled "I Keep Six Honest Serving Men."[*]

I Keep Six Honest Serving Men

I keep six honest serving-men
    (They taught me all I knew);
  Their names are What and Why and When
    And How and Where and Who.
I send them over land and sea,
    I send them east and west;
  But after they have worked for me,
    I give them all a rest.

I let them rest from nine till five.
    For I am busy then,
As well as breakfast, lunch, and tea,
    For they are hungry men:
But different folk have different views:
    I know a person small—
She keeps ten million serving-men,
    Who get no rest at all!

She sends 'em abroad on her own affairs,
    From the second she opens her eyes—
One million Hows, two million Wheres,
    And seven million Whys![†]

---

[*] Rudyard Kipling. Retrieved from http://www.goodreads.com/author/quotes/6989.Rudyard_Kipling?page=4
[†] Jalic, Inc. (2014).

The Five Ws and One H in the poem are considered to be a problem-solving method referred to as the "Kipling Method." This method helps explore problems by using the six questions as a starting point in getting answers.

Assign Project Staff

The process of assigning the project staff consists of obtaining the agile team (i.e., developers, Product Owner, and agile leader) necessary to complete project activities. The agile team needs to be cross-functional and capable of working under time-boxed constraints to deliver a high-quality product. Value to the customer must be built quickly and delivered frequently. In addition, the product's quality needs to be validated by means of verification and validation activities.

The agile team has a number of responsibilities that need to be achieved. The desired characteristics of an effective agile team include but are not limited to the following traits:[*]

- *Self-managed:* The agile team should be able to function effectively in a self-regulating environment.
- *Colocated:* Agile teams work better when everyone is physically in the same location.
- *Small team:* The agile team should "typically" not have more than 6-10 members.
- *Single backlog:* The agile team should work from only one backlog.
- *Commitment:* The agile team should be committed to building and delivering a high-value product.
- *Communication:* The team must be effective with face-to-face communications.
- *Accommodate change:* The agile team should be able to embrace changes and accommodate unplanned work.
- *Create reasonable estimates:* The team must be able to create reasonable estimates for the work that they agree to complete and must deliver what they agree upon.
- *Continuous improvement:* The team must continuously find ways to improve its performance.

---

[*] Leffingwell, LLC. (2014a).

- *Cross-functional:* The team members must be cross-functional and have the capability to perform in multiple roles as needed.
- *Sustainable pace:* The agile project team must be able to maintain a sustainable pace throughout the project.

Develop Project Backlog

The agile team's main focus is to plan to deliver high-value features as early as possible and at the same time avoid or mitigate risks. During the planning phase, the product backlog is prioritized based on the product's features that have the greatest value and/or the highest risk levels. *Epics* (large user stories) are created during the beginning of the projects when requirements (user stories) are very high level[*] and have not yet been decomposed enough for the development team to work with. Because the epics are originally too large during project planning, they are broken down, clarified, and prioritized to create the initial product backlog for the project. The Product Owner is responsible for prioritizing the user stories in the backlog.

Create Estimates

There are many techniques that are used on agile teams to create estimates. We discuss several of the most common estimating techniques.

Affinity Estimation[†]

This is the process of positioning the requirements into groupings. On the agile project, this method is used to place similar sized user stories together in the same group so that a proportional view of the estimates can be obtained. When the team places the user stories into groups based on size, it provides an opportunity to see if they have been accurate with similar estimates. This technique ensures that the size of a story point remains consistent throughout their estimates. The approach for this type of estimation is to create columns on a task board for different requirements and then place the user stories in the columns that match the "size."

---

[*] SCRUMstudy. (2013).
[†] Griffiths, M. (2012).

TABLE 8.2

Affinity Estimation

Story Size	1	2	3	4	5	6	7	8	9	10
	▣▣▣▣▣▣	▣▣▣	▣	▣▣▣	▣▣	▣	▣▣▣	▣	▣▣	▣

TABLE 8.3

Fist of Five

Number	Meaning	Description
1.	One Finger	Team member disagrees with the group's conclusion and has major concerns.
2.	Two Fingers	Team member disagrees with the group's conclusion and wants to discuss minor issues.
3.	Three Fingers	Team member is not sure but wants to go with the group's consensus and conclusion.
4.	Four Fingers	Team member agrees with the group's conclusion and wants to discuss minor issues.
5.	Five Fingers	Team member agrees wholeheartedly with the group's conclusion.

This will determine if the story point sizing method is valid. Table 8.2 shows an example of how this process should be conducted.

1. *Fist of Five:** This agile estimation technique is based on gaining group consensus. A discussion or proposition is presented to the team and each member is asked to cast a vote based on a scale of one to five. Team members use their fingers to display their votes. In addition to gaining consensus, this technique also facilitates discussion among the group. After a team discussion, a united decision is made. The number of fingers raised by each member indicates the level of agreement and/or need for further discussion. Table 8.3 outlines the meaning of each raised finger.
2. *Ideal Time:* This technique is based on estimating and omitting interruptions. For example, in an eight-hour business day, all eight hours

---

* SCRUMstudy. (2013).

are not available for working. Lunch, breaks, or time out of the office are not counted in the estimates. Ideal time is not realistic as to what happens in the real world, however, it keeps the estimation process very simple.* This estimation process is very accurate because it only includes actual work time and nothing more. When estimating a user story based on ideal time, work time is calculated based on "no disruptions."

3. *Story Points:* A story point is simply a "relative measurement of work." The main idea of using story points for agile estimation is to discontinue calculations based on hours worked per week. Why is this so? Hours per week fluctuate for many agile team members and using this measurement is often not realistic. Story point estimation takes very little time, is flexible, and can be easily modified. Agile teams typically create their own definitions for their story points and each team has the freedom to determine the appropriate story point sizes. For clarification, baselines are created after the story point value had been defined and agreed upon by the development team. Once the story point value is established, it will not change for agile iterations. Story points do not necessarily need to add up to a whole when they are broken down. The level of complexity, work effort, and risk should be considered when determining the number of points assigned to a story. Lastly, story point calculations should make sense in that 1 + 1 = 2. This means that two one-point stories should equal out to roughly a two-point story.

Still not sure what story points are? Let's continue our discussion. As some of us may have experienced, estimating work can be unpleasant, time consuming, and difficult. Readers should recall that agile methods are about simplicity and story points were designed to make things simple. Story points are based upon using a comparative approach to estimating where we base new activity estimates against work that has already been completed. Basically, we are comparing new estimates with prior estimates which is in actuality a very good practice. Readers must understand that the story point estimates are perceived to be better than hours per week estimates on the agile project. Why is this the case? According to Griffiths (2012) when estimating in hours, this can create a fake ceiling. Estimating in hours has the potential to create issues for some workers who have

---

* Griffiths, M. (2012).

heavy demands on their time and are never able to provide 40 hours of actual project work per week. There are several things that readers need to keep in mind when working with story points.

- The development team is responsible for its own story point sizing definitions. For instance, the team may agree that one story point is equal to one hour; or one story point is equal to one day, and so on. It is strictly up to what the team decides upon.
- The story point estimate should include all activities. Nothing should be left out or added in after the story point has been defined.
- In the case where a story point is decomposed, the total of the individual units is not required to match. This means that when epics are broken down into user stories, it is not required that the totals of broken-down user stories add up to the original size of the epic. Got that? As an example, if an epic is sized as 10 story points and it is broken down into three user stories that equal 2, 3, and 1, respectively, it is OK that the total does not equal 10 and this only applies during the decomposition process!
- Story point sizes should be relative. Simply put, a three-point story point should equal approximately three times the work effort of one story point.
- Story points should include work effort, risk, and level of complexity. The entire time that is needed to do the work should be included in a story point.

4. *Wideband Delphi:* According to the *PMBOK® Guide* (2013), the Delphi technique is used to gain agreement among a group of experts.* The wideband Delphi technique is used to gain group consensus for a particular estimation approach.† This tactic gathers a group of experts and asks them to anonymously make estimates. Anonymity is used as a precaution against bias. A wideband Delphi session is initiated with identifying the problem at hand. The project is then broken down into practicable "pieces" in order to be manageable by the group. For example, a problem specification is first created, assumptions and constraints are discussed, and a process for moving forward with successive estimation meetings is developed.

---

* PMI. (2013).
† Griffiths, M. (2012).

The team is allowed to ask questions openly prior to providing estimates. A meeting facilitator collects the estimates from the group based on "rounds" (number of meetings). After several rounds of estimations, the group of experts should begin to reach a consensus on the estimates provided. All of the experts must reach agreement on the final list of tasks and their estimations. The wideband Delphi technique is effective because it considers feedback from all of the experts. The collaborative nature of this technique increases the buy-in phase so that consensus can be ultimately reached by all.

Cost Estimation

In order to determine cost estimates for the agile project, there are several calculation steps that need to take place. A discussion of this process follows:

1. Calculate the size of the project based on the total number of story points.
   a. This can be done using planning poker or another estimation technique.
2. Calculate the amount of work to be completed on the project in person-days. We can use ideal time (previously discussed in this chapter). Person-days can then be reduced to hours.
   a. This calculation is done by adding up the availability percentages for all team members and then dividing this result by the total number of team members. For example, if there are four teaming members (Tom, Bruce, Donna, and Mary), the individual availability percentage for each is (100%, 100%, 85%, and 50%). We add these percentages and then divide by 4 to get: ((100 + 100 + 85 + 50)/4 = 84%). If the total ideal time is 800 days to the complete project, we divide 800 days by 0.84 (800/.84 = 952 person-days). If we have four people doing the work, we calculate the work per person (952/4 = 238) person-days.
3. Determine the project schedule based on the calculated person-days. In this step, we need to take into consideration dependencies or constraints that may affect the number of actual person-days. We now need to translate person-days into months. There are 21 working days (on average) in a month, so we calculate (238/21 = 11.33) months to complete the project.

TABLE 8.4

Total Project Costs

Name	Rate ($)	Total Hours	Total Costs ($)
Tom	75	1,903	142,725.00
Bruce	89	1,903	169,367.00
Donna	87	1,903	165,561.00
Mary	72	1,903	137,016.00
Total Project Costs			614,669.00

4. Calculate the total costs of the project with labor rates and other associated costs.
    a. The formula to calculate is: total cost = (time × resource rate) + (other project costs).
    b. We need the hourly rates for each of the team members (Tom, Bruce, Donna, and Mary). Each of their hourly rates is ($75, $89, $87, and $72), and working 8 hours per day, with an average of 21 days is (8 × 21 = 168) hours per month. Next we calculate the number of project hours, (11.33 × 168 = 1903).
    c. We now plug in the labor costs for each team member. See Table 8.4 for total project costs ($614,669.00).

Develop Road Map with Story Mapping

This is the final process in the agile project initiation phase. The agile term *story map* is used to describe the method for selecting and grouping product features that are going into a particular release. Story maps show the priority levels of features based on how they have been classified. For example, *backbone, walking skeleton,* or *additional features* are classification terms that can be translated into priority levels high, medium, or low. When product features are placed on the story map according to their relative level of importance and order, the customer's priorities are then put in parallel to what the development team can actually deliver. The end result is that the product's releases can be identified on the road map as a result of defining the story map. For additional clarification, the story map shows the importance of features based on their order (left to right). The road map, on the other hand, shows in which releases the stories will be. At first glance, the product road map and the story map may appear to be very similar, however, just the opposite is true. The product road map is used to illustrate the product's releases and the functionality to be developed within each release. In contrast, the product's story map shows how the features can be grouped for a release. All critical functionality for the system is labeled as the backbone stories and the walking skeleton stories represent those that can create the smallest possible working system. The third and final group of features remaining is prioritized based on their relative importance to the agile team.[*]

PLAN RELEASE

A release is simply a distribution of the product outside the agile team. This means that the software is released to the end user. The release plan is developed to communicate when the software will be released and what functionality is to be contained within the release. The customer typically decides when the product will be released, however, the agile team is permitted to provide its input. Releases can be date or functionality driven. The release plan is developed for planning purposes and to provide important information to the stakeholders. There are three activities that are typically undertaken during the release planning process. A discussion of these activities follows:

1. Breakdown epics
2. Estimate stories with poker planning
3. Create release plan

Breakdown Epics

Epics are large user stories that need to be further broken down. The breakdown process results in smaller, more manageable, user stories. There is no right or wrong way to break down an epic but a hierarchical approach is recommended with the end result being a task that is estimated by the development team and used to build a product feature. Starting from the epic, user stories are created. From a single user story, several tasks are

---

[*] Griffiths, M. (2012).

created. The hierarchical process for breaking down the epic into smaller components follows:

- Epic 1
- Epic 2
  - User Story 1
    - Task 1
    - Task 2
    - Task 3
  - User Story 2
    - Task 1
    - Task 2
  - User Story 3
    - Task 1

Estimate Stories with Poker Planning

This estimation technique is based on obtaining team consensus to estimate the size of user stories. Planning poker starts with all team members being assigned a single deck of poker cards. The cards in each deck are numbered using the Fibonacci* sequence (0, 1, 1, 2, 3, 5, 8, 13, 21, 34, …). The Fibonacci sequence is calculated by adding the two previous numbers to get the next number in the sequence (0 + 1 = 1, 1 + 1 = 2, 1 + 2 = 3, etc.). The numbers represent the estimated level of complexity based on effort and time. The Product Owner leads the estimation game and presents each user story to the development team. Each agile team member evaluates the user story and attempts to understand the complexity associated with it. Each developer then selects a card from his or her deck that describes his or her estimation for the user story being discussed. If a consensus is reached by the majority of the team, then that estimate is used for that particular user story. In the case where there is no agreement on the user story estimation, each team member provides reasons for the selections. The estimation process is repeated until a consensus is reached on the number representing the estimation.[†] The final number is recorded on the user story as the story point value.

---

* MathisFun (2013).
[†] SCRUMstudy (2013).

Create Release Plan

The first step in creating an agile release plan is to determine what needs to be accomplished in terms of goals and objectives. Creating the release plan is not done blindly; the business goals and the team's velocity (capacity) is very relevant during this planning process because the team's capability drives the release planning and outcome. Speaking of the team's velocity, this number is determined by how many story points the development team can complete during an iteration. It would take several iterations for the team to obtain an average number of story points that they can complete and this means that the team velocity is only established after such time. The priority of the user stories is also an important factor with regard to what goes into the release plan. A consensus must be reached in terms of the goals of the release plan. The development team must make a realistic commitment as to the amount of work that can be completed for each planned release.

ITERATION 0

The goal of iteration 0 is simply to prepare for iteration 1. According to Scott Ambler & Associates (2012),[*] approximately the first week or so of an agile project is considered to be iteration 0. This iteration is considered to be the warmup or the inception phase of the agile project. The following events take place during this time frame:

- The project is initiated.
- Support and funding are established for the project.
- Stakeholders are active and participating in the project.
- The team is established.
- The agile environment is created.
- The initial system architecture is modeled.

---

[*] Scott Ambler & Associates. (2012).

There are two main activities that are conducted during iteration 0:

1. Architectural spikes.
2. Prepare for iteration 1.

A detailed discussion of these activities follows.

Architectural Spikes[*]

Architectural spikes are iterations that prove specific technological approaches. Risk-based spikes are periods of work that are used to mitigate risks. Spikes are included in release planning. An architectural spike can be either functional or technical in nature and it represents a story that is used to validate the exploration of an idea, a design, or research. The goal of a spike is to acquire information that is required to mitigate the risk of a technology-based approach, gain understanding of a particular product requirement, or validate an estimate for a task(s). A functional spike is conducted to analyze combinations of functional behavior that may need to be broken down or analyzed for risk complexity. This is done so that the correct implementation decisions can be made. In contrast, the technical spike is conducted to validate design considerations. Spikes are implemented during the end of an iteration and are owned by specific team members. In simple terms, a spike is used to eliminate risk within a particular user story. It is important to understand that a spike is not adding value for the customer and should be used cautiously. On the other hand, if an opportunity can be created from a spike, it would be considered to be adding value.

For clarification, an architectural spike is an iteration designed to prove a technological approach and spikes are work done to reduce risks.[†] There is a concept called a *risk-based* spike. This type of spike is done so the development team can determine whether a particular technological issue is feasible. The goal of this type of spike is risk reduction, possible cost reduction, and to improve the chances that the project will be successful. Risk-based spikes are used to conduct experiments so that high-risk components of the project can be fully understood and their impacts mitigated. If the experiment's results show feasibility, the risk is eliminated.

---

[*] Leffingwell, LLC. (2014b).
[†] Griffiths, M. (2012).

This results in the overall project having a lower risk ranking. If the results of the experiment are not feasible, then a different approach is used. If all experiments show results that are not feasible, then this would mean this particular project has a high failure rate and should be abandoned.

Risk-based spikes are used to validate new technologies or those that are unfamiliar. These spikes are done early in the project so that development efforts will not waste money and time in the event that the technology is determined to be too risky.

Prepare for Iteration 1 during Iteration 0

During the preparation for iteration 1, the development team will need to compute its team velocity, excluding downtime (vacations, sick leave, etc.). The main goal of iteration 0 is to prepare the next iteration's (iteration 1 in this case) user story details. This involves the utilization of several tools and techniques including but not limited to: creating use cases, activity diagrams, data models, sequence diagrams, acceptance tests, business cases, and identifying data fields.* Keep in mind that the agile project is not designed for much up-front planning because this activity is done throughout the entire project. Up-front planning is not done on the agile project because there is very little static information available early in the project. Details on the agile project are discovered along the way and the team must make adjustments as they are warranted. The best way to describe the planning for the agile project is "adaptive." The team adapts as it proceeds. See Table 8.5 for a high-level view of the iterations as they relate to releases.

TABLE 8.5

Iteration Cycles

	Iteration Cycles									
Iteration 0	I1	I2	I3	I4	I5	I6	I7	I8		
		R1		R2		R3		R4		R5

Note: I = Iteration, R = Release.

---

* Griffiths, M. (2012).

This concludes our discussion of iteration 0. Keep in mind that every agile project is unique and there may be variation in the activities based on the needs and objectives of the project. We now begin our discussion of the preparation of iterations 1 through N (where N is the total number of iterations in a given release).

ITERATION PLANNING 1–N (WHERE N IS THE TOTAL NUMBER OF ITERATIONS IN A RELEASE)

Iteration planning involves deciding upon the high-priority user stories that will bring the most value to the customer. The iteration planning goal should be established (i.e., the number of user stories to be completed during the iteration), however, if the project is a first, the team velocity may not be established yet. Remember, the team's velocity can only be established after they have completed several iterations and have obtained an average number of story points that can be accurately defined as its capacity (velocity). In any event, the development team is empowered to decide on the number of user stories for the iteration and they must discuss their recommendation with the customer.

During the iteration planning meetings, the customer (or Product Owner) has the ultimate responsibility for prioritizing the product backlog and indicating to the team which user stories she would like to see in the iteration. The agile team will then select a set of user stories from the backlog that they feel can be completed in the iteration. The customer establishes the priorities for the iteration, however, the development team has the final say on the amount of work they believe they can complete for the iteration. An iteration backlog is the plan that the development team works from to deliver the product for the iteration. Iterations 1–N are considered to be development iterations and the goal is to deliver system functionality that meets or exceeds the customer's expectations. The agile team delivers the product in increments. Test-driven development (TDD) activities, an XP concept explained in Chapter 3, are conducted to confirm the validity of the user stories. The team works collaboratively and the product is internally deployed for acceptance. Stakeholders are very participative and provide feedback as deemed necessary. Keep in mind that iterations are time-boxed into approximately two-week time frames. There is never an infinite amount of time to complete an iteration.

Iteration R

The purpose of iteration R is to deploy the product to the production environment. This iteration is separated from iterations 1–N (where N is the total number of iterations). Why does this separation occur? It occurs so that the development team can continue to build functionality for the next release and in order for the current release to be moved to production. Keep in mind that in the case of a final release, there would not be any continued development activities. The following activities occur during iteration R. The development team, of course, takes care of all iteration R activities:

- Complete project documentation.
- Formal testing (security, performance, integration, or regression).
- Deploy the software to production.
- Celebration, Celebration, Celebration!!!!!

Coding

The Agile Manifesto and its guiding principle state: "*Build projects around motivated individuals; give them the environment and support that they need and trust them to get the job done.*" According to Ambysoft, Inc. (2013),* a common best practice on the agile team is to provide the development team with *sandboxes* in which to develop code. What is a sandbox? It's just a fancy name for a respected technical development environment with a "well-defined scope." How's that for fancy? Ambysoft further indicates that the sandbox reduces risk because it protects against technical errors. There is less worry on the agile development team because access is limited, which results in fewer mishaps. Specific categories of sandboxes include:

- *Development Sandbox:* Development environment where only the development team has access to develop the code for the product.
- *Integration Sandbox:* Build environment from which each project team works. Code is integrated from all of the development activities to ensure it will work well when integrated.

---

* Ambysoft, Inc. (2013).

- *Demo Sandbox:* Working code environment where demos can be carried out for the client.
- *Preproduction/Test Sandbox:* Staging environment that is generally a replication of the live production environment. Systems testing is executed in this environment prior to the release to production.
- *Production:* This is the live environment for the completed product.

Execute Acceptance Tests

The purpose of the acceptance test in the agile environment is to ensure that the product meets the requirements from the customer's perspective. These tests are designed to verify the functionality of the product based on actual demonstrations. On the agile project, the customer or their representative performs the actual testing to ensure that the product performs as expected. In addition, acceptance testing (or user acceptance testing) is executed during development iterations.[*]

Many agile projects conduct what is known as acceptance test-driven development (ATDD).[†] This type of testing focuses on the business requirement rather than the code. Test cases are created prior to code development and are designed to demonstrate the product's functionality for the customer's acceptance. Prior to the creation of an acceptance test case based on a user story from the backlog, the customer clarifies the desired behavior. There are four steps to the acceptance test case and demonstration process.

1. The requirements are discussed and the customer is asked questions so that the proper acceptance test can be developed.
2. The acceptance test cases are entered into an acceptance testing tool.
3. Code is developed and acceptance test cases are attached and executed. If the code is attached to the correct tests, the expectation is that the test will pass; otherwise, if not attached correctly, the tests will fail.
4. The development team demonstrates the software to the customer using the automated acceptance tests.

---

[*] Scrum Alliance. (2013).
[†] Griffiths, M. (2012).

Create Test Cases

Agile projects use test-driven development to create test cases. Test-driven development requires that the development team envision how the product's functionality works prior to the creation of the code. Tests are then typically written in a unit testing language such as JUnit. The initial test will fail merely because the code would not have been created yet for the functionality. The development team writes code and runs the test case until the code has successfully passed the test.

Execute Automated Testing

Automated tests are used for test-driven development and acceptance test-driven development. TDD, an XP concept, is used to implement coding and testing cycles to ensure that the code functions as intended. The test is developed before the code. When the code actually passes the test, the functionality is considered to be completed. On the first run of the test, failure occurs because the code has not yet been developed. A cycle of test execution and writing code is repeated until the test passes. Development efforts continue in the case where additional functionality is needed; otherwise when all tests pass, the code is then refactored. ATDD focuses on the business requirement rather than the code. This means that these types of automated tests are used to demonstrate that functionality is acceptable to the customer. These tests are also written prior to the development of the code. TDD and ATDD have been reiterated in this book because they are important concepts of agile methods.

Definition of "Done"

Agile methods place great emphasis on defining what "done" means and having all stakeholders (i.e., executive management, sponsor, managers, agile project team, users, etc.) agree on what the word looks like for the project. A simple but effective way to define what "done" means is to document the criteria that define what is meant so that everyone is clear on its meaning. *Done* could describe the following conditions or a combination of conditions such as:

- All stakeholders are in agreement that everything is done.
- All issues have been resolved.

- Customer signoff has occurred on all user stories for an iteration and/or release.
- Testing is completed.

To summarize, the criteria for done should be agreed upon, recorded, and approved by all stakeholders.

Answer Client's Questions for Sign-Off

At the end of the development iterations, the customer and project stakeholders gather for a meeting to review the prioritized backlog items. The product's functionality is validated and participants ask questions and provide feedback. The customer has the final say as to the acceptance or rejection of a requirement (user story from the backlog), however, the decision is based on the previously established acceptance criteria. The customer does not have the authority to change the agreed-upon acceptance criteria once the iteration is underway. Once the customer agrees that the user story is done, the prioritized backlog item is signed off on either verbally or in writing based on the practices of the customer organization.

Prepare Stories for Next Iteration

The preparation of user stories is simply to outline requirements for the product's functionality. In the case of Scrum, for example, a user story should provide the following information:*

- *Who?:* Represents the user role executing the functionality
- *What?:* Represents what the user role should be able to perform in the system
- *Why?:* Represents the reason why the user needs to perform the desired function in the system

See Table 8.6 for an example of a user story based on the Who, What, Why format described above.

---

* SCRUMstudy. (2013).

TABLE 8.6

User Stories Format

As a <role>, I should be able to <requirement> so that <benefit>

User Story Example:
(1) As a customer, I should be able to send an e-mail to the bank so that I can communicate quickly and easily.
(2) As a vendor, I should be able to create an estimate so that I can show the client how much iterations will cost.

Daily Standup Meeting

As discussed in Chapter 3 under the Scrum framework, the daily standup meeting is time-boxed to a maximum of 15 minutes. One may contemplate how a meeting can be conducted in such a short time frame. The answer is that each team member (typically just the development team) is asked three questions:

1. What have you worked on since we last met?
2. What do you plan to complete today?
3. Are there any obstacles in the way of completing your work?

Update Burndown/Burnup Charts

Both the Burndown and Burnup Charts are used to show how much progress has been made on the agile project. The Burndown Chart reveals the amount of remaining work that needs to be completed and the Burnup Chart reflects what has been delivered for the product. These particular charts can be tailored to show progress based on time or the number of iterations. When using iterations as a measure of progress, story points show scope levels per iteration. When using the amount of time as a measure, then these charts show the approximate amount of time remaining. Important to note is that these charts can be created in Microsoft Excel.

Iteration Retrospective

Many of the agile methods conduct retrospectives as a way to learn, to reflect, and to provide the foundations for making improvements in the agile process. The retrospective meeting occurs after a single iteration and the agile team members convene to discuss ways to improve their techniques. A benefit of the retrospective meeting is the fact that it occurs during the agile project and there is time to implement the lessons learned information on the current project. The process of reviewing lessons learned throughout the project is very beneficial because the team has the opportunity to:

- Improve its performance by increasing productivity.
- Improve on knowledge attainment by sharing information.
- Improve on product quality by undermining the cause of defects.
- Improve on making processes more efficient which in turn will increase team capacity.

The iteration retrospective is typically time-boxed for two hours and it is process driven with five major phases.*

1. *Establish the stage:* Focusing the participants on discussing the events of the last completed iteration. Encourage the team to speak up and remain engaged throughout the meeting. Give everyone a chance to contribute. Create a master list of issues for the team to work from. Prepare for the next step in the process.
2. *Compile the data:* Compiling the data based on the events that occurred during the iteration.
3. *Create insights:* Giving the participants an opportunity to evaluate the information gathered (brainstorming, etc.).
4. *Decide upon what needs to be done:* Giving the team an opportunity to decide on what they need to change for the next iteration based on the events from the last completed iteration.
5. *Close the retrospective meeting:* Reflections, expressions of thanks to each other, document and validate any team ideas as appropriate. Discuss what went well, what went wrong, and so on.

This concludes our overview of iterations 1–*N* and the activities that occur during these phases of the agile project. Once all the iterations have been completed for a release, there is an option to begin a new release and the iterations begin once again. After all the releases have been successfully completed, the product is delivered to the customer. We now turn

---

* Griffiths, M. (2012).

our attention to what happens after the agile project is complete. As in traditional project management, the agile project must be properly closed out. A discussion of close-out activities follows.

CLOSE-OUT ACTIONS

A main focus of conducting close-out activities for the agile project should include a celebration for the purpose of showing appreciation to the team members for completing a successful project and for formally ending the project. Celebrations are also good for keeping morale levels high among the team members during this transition period. During this stage of the agile project, documentation should be finalized for administrative and financial reporting requirements as applicable. A "project retrospective" should be conducted for the purposes of documenting and sharing information from the team's knowledge base. Any lessons learned information, both good and bad, should be shared by the project team so that others may use this information to learn from on future projects.

CHAPTER SUMMARY

Agile project management is an iterative and incremental process that is used for new product development, information technology, engineering, and the like. Agile methods are very flexible, transparent, and adaptive. The agile project management process supports changes and consistent stakeholder involvement. The project management role is shared between the entire agile team which is in contrast to a single project manager in the traditional project management role. What a difference!

9

Agile Value

Chapter 9 begins our discussion of an important agile concept: *value*. Agile methods are all about delivering value. What exactly do we mean by value? As previously mentioned in Chapter 1, we are referring to business value, a concept that pertains to different variations of value that define the strength and health of a company for the long term. Business value encompasses several types (stakeholder value, increased profits). Projects are taken on to increase business value. This includes producing some type of benefit or improvements to existing services. A company must consider choices and make decisions that maximize business value and reduce risks. A risk does not add value and it must be managed. To summarize, a business must maximize value coming in and minimize value going out of the firm in order to remain profitable. For the purposes of our discussion and in contrast to traditional project management, we are referring to negative risks only.

CALCULATING VALUE

Readers should recall that we discussed what we mean by the word "value" in Chapter 1. A common way to calculate value without bias is to calculate a return on investment (ROI), internal rate of return (IRR), or the net present value (NPV). Each of these three formulas can be relatively easy to calculate with the help of Microsoft Excel. The meanings of these formulas are as follows:

- Net present value (NPV): When choosing between several projects to take on, the one with the highest NPV should be selected over the others.

- Return on investment (ROI): The project with the highest ROI should be selected.
- Internal rate of return (IRR): Select the project with the highest IRR.

Readers may be aware that value can be intangible, however, the author is referring to tangible value that is subjective and cannot easily be disputed.

PLAN VALUE

When planning an agile project, the focus should be on value. The work that needs to be done on the project should be prioritized based on its business value. This means that the user stories adding the most value should be added in early iterations rather than later. High-risk user stories should be addressed in the same way because risk can reduce value. We want to ensure that we maximize value by handling high-risk items early in the project to lessen the impact of those that are non-value-added. Readers must once again understand that the author is referring to negative risks in this instance.

ADAPTABILITY AND VALUE

The logic behind adaptability in the agile environment is that projects should be at all times open to accepting changes. In traditional project management, changes must go through a formal process in order to be evaluated and approved for incorporation into the project. This would not be the case for the agile project as change is expected and embraced. As mentioned in Chapter 1, the acceptance of change does not automatically imply that "anything goes" on the agile project. With regard to change and adaptability, the idea is to accept changes that increase the amount of value for the customer.

Adaptive Planning

According to the Declaration of Interdependence (DOI) from Chapter 2, *"we increase return on investment by making continuous flow of value our focus."* The agile project must deliver a constant flow of value to the customer.

Agile methods are all about delivering the maximum amount of value to the customer and minimizing non-value-added activities. Adaptive planning is an agile concept that suggests plans will more than likely change (and they always do) and it is wiser to plan on replanning and adapting as things change. Again, this is in contrast to the traditional project management approach where the development of plans is a required process.

Again, we refer back to the DOI from Chapter 2: "*we expect uncertainty and manage for it through iterations, anticipation, and adaptation.*" We are referring to changes on the agile project. There is a high level of change on the agile project and the expectation is that the plan will need to be adapted as we proceed. We have now come to a familiar concept that is shared with both traditional and agile projects. This term is *progressive elaboration*, which means to add more detail as it becomes available. This would mean that planning should consist of continually making updates throughout the project. In the agile environment, plans are updated throughout the iterations.

Agile versus Traditional Changes

As we have seen throughout this book thus far, agile and traditional project management practices are frequently dissimilar. The agile world focuses on experiments and demonstrations that reveal hidden project requirements. As new information is uncovered, replanning becomes necessary. Contrary to traditional project management and its extensive planning efforts, there is very little up-front planning on the agile project because planning is done throughout the project. Changes and adjustments are customary on the agile project, whereas the traditional project views changes as cumbersome and often unwelcome.

Minimally Marketable Features

In terms of a release, there are certain requirements that must be satisfied in order to provide value to the end user. *Minimally marketable feature* is a term that must apply to any release of the product for customer use. This means that a release of the product must contain the minimally marketable features possible and is not representative of the complete product.

Tailoring and Value

A DOI principle states that "*we improve effectiveness and reliability through situational specific strategies, processes, and practices.*" This brings us to the concept of *tailoring*. The author expects that many experienced project managers are quite familiar with this terminology. The iteration or project retrospectives provide the opportunity to reflect on what works, what does not work, what should be done differently, and what needs to be improved. When reflecting on areas that may need to be enhanced, it is these types of situations which result in tailoring, which is considered to be a form of adaptation.

DELIVER VALUE

Value is delivered when an agile project is executed. The team delivers through the process of maximizing value and minimizing non-value-added activities. Any type of wastefulness is considered to be in the category of non-value-adding activities. Following are examples of wasteful activities that should be considered when attempting to maximize value. These activities should be avoided as much as possible. The following list includes but is not limited to the following:

- *Unfinished work:* Started but not finished; this is considered to be wasteful.
- *Unnecessary processes:* Work that does not add value; irrelevant work does not add value.
- *Bugs:* Faulty software or artifacts; this is considered to be rework and it is considered to be wasteful.
- *Noncollocated communication efforts:* Remote teams; this would require a greater level of effort to communicate if the team is not colocated. There is some waste involved.
- *Extra features:* Not required or good to have features; wasting time doing unneeded work.
- *Waiting around:* Delays for approvals or signoffs; wasting time by waiting.
- *Switching projects:* Working on more than one project; multitasking on multiple projects. Agile team members should be focused on one project at a time if possible.

Iterative delivery is a good way to maximize value on the agile project. Increments of the product are demonstrated and delivered as working software. Recall that working software is the highest priority of agile methods. Value is delivered early which results in the obtainment of a fast return on investment.

Using Software or Task Boards to Deliver Value

On the agile project, a common tool that is used to display the project status is the task board. Traditional project management uses software such as MS Project to manage its scheduling requirements. Some believe that using scheduling software is not practical on the agile project and here's why:

- Scheduling software shows layers of tasks that are often lengthy and interdependent.
- Scheduling software may be viewed as being too complex for agile projects.
- Scheduling software is sometimes viewed as primarily the project manager's tool and not necessarily a team tool.

Task (or white) boards are the simple alternative to scheduling software on the agile project. From Chapter 7, we have discussed the three columns on the task board: (1) To Do, (2) In Progress, and (3) Done. This is a simple, yet visual scheduling way to show the work status of an iteration quickly. The benefits of task boards include:

- Agile projects have a preference for low technology, high visibility tools.
- Simplicity is always the best approach for the agile project. The task board is very simple in comparison with scheduling software.
- The accuracy of data on the task board is visible for the entire agile team and all stakeholders to see. It is perceived that data on the task board will be more accurate than data entered into a scheduling tool.
- With a scheduling tool, charts and graphs are not always accessible for all project team members. In contrast, the task board is visible to all at any time.

ANALYZING AND DETERMINING VALUE

In order to analyze and deliver the maximum value for the customer properly, we must reflect on the business value of our efforts and then take the appropriate action. We must focus on business value throughout the entire agile project and every work component, practice, procedure, or

TABLE 9.1

Analyzing and Determining Value

Item Description	Feature #1 ($)	Feature #2 ($)
Benefit	15,000	8,000
Development cost	−5,000	−2,000
Delivery cost	−1,000	−500
Total value	9,000	5,500

effort must add value. In addition, we must focus our efforts on delivering the highest value items before those with lower value. All costing factors (such as coding and distribution) associated with value must be included. This is referred to as comparing the benefits versus the costs to calculate the value. See Table 9.1 for an example of analyzing and determining value.

Another factor that we need to consider when analyzing value is that we cannot always just focus only on high-value items. We need to consider that some intermediate-level items can add value faster than a high-value item, which will result in delivering high value quicker. In other cases, high-value features may need low-value items in order to function properly. This is a codependent situation that may need to be addressed after the analysis process has been undertaken. The bottom line is that the agile team must understand how to determine what is actually high value and what is not.

VALUE PRIORITIZATION

User stories (requirements) must be prioritized based on value as perceived by the customer. This in turn means that the customer must be a part of the discussions during the prioritization process. There are several techniques that are used to prioritize requirements from the customer's perception and a discussion follows. These techniques are referred to as prioritization schemes:[*]

1. *Monopoly Money:* This scheme is played somewhat like the Monopoly game in that the customer is asked to divide the money up among the product's features. During this process, the high-priority items are

---

[*] Griffiths, M. (2012).

discovered. The monopoly money should be limited to high-value product features to ensure effectiveness in the prioritization game.

2. *100-Point Model:* This prioritization scheme is based upon use cases. Stakeholders are given 100 points to vote for the high-priority requirements. The higher the points for a feature are, the higher the priority level.

3. *MoSCoW Prioritization Scheme:* This prioritization scheme is based on the letters in the name of the scheme where: (Note that the letter O is not used.)

   - **M** stands for *Must have*
     - Priority 1—Very High
   - **S** stands for *Should have*
     - Priority 2—High
   - **C** stands for *Could have*
     - Priority 3—Moderate
   - **W** stands for *Would like to have, but not now*
     - Priority 4—Low

The meanings of these letters are pretty straightforward and represent the priority levels of the requirements. There are other prioritization schemes, however, we limit our discussion to the three mentioned above. The idea is to use a method that the customer is comfortable with when prioritizing the user stories based on value. Readers must understand that any prioritization scheme can be used; even one that is as simple as High, Medium or Low.

CONFIRM VALUE

Value is confirmed on the agile project by means of demonstrating the product increments to the customer and other stakeholders. These demonstrations take place as simulations or prototypes. Regardless of the methods, during these demonstrations, requirements are clarified and the customer is given the chance to accept or reject the software that has been presented. In certain instances, these demos result in the acknowledgment that additional requirements are needed or the existing requirements are enhanced (functionality added to an existing user story).

TRACK AND REPORT VALUE

The final value-related action is to track and report value. On the agile project, the idea is to make sure that the project stays on track and information gets communicated to the stakeholders. This information is covered in detail in Chapter 7 as "Agile Tracking and Reporting."

CHAPTER SUMMARY

Delivering value to the business is a main feature of agile methods. Most decisions on the agile project are focused around the amount of value that the project can create. Value-driven delivery must be maximized for the customer at all times and any non-valued-added activities and events such as risks must be managed or eliminated. It is really that simple. The agile project should at all times add value.

10

Agile Risk Management

A risk is considered to be an uncertain event(s) that has the potential to contribute to the success or failure of a project. Positive risks are defined as opportunities and threats are risks that can affect the project in a negative way. In the agile world, adverse risks are of greater concern because they have the potential to have an adverse impact on value added for the customer. This is not to say that opportunities are overlooked; threats, however, have a higher priority level. The author believes that changes represent opportunities to add value for the customer and are eagerly added to the product as they are revealed.

Risks should be managed throughout the entire project. This means that risks need to be identified, evaluated, and responded to based upon probability and impact of the risk. User stories that are identified as being high-risk items should be addressed as early as possible. This means that these items should be included in early iterations rather than later ones. Threats should be proactively attacked before they affect the project as risks. The iterative nature of agile methods functions in such a way that risks can be addressed very early in the project through the iterations. Threat reduction should occur during the selection of specific product features or user stories. Just as in traditional project management practices, risks on the agile project can be evaluated based on their probability and impact. The severity level of risks can be calculated as follows:

$$\text{Probability} \times \text{Impact} = \text{Severity}$$

Table 10.1 is an example of how risks are identified in terms of impact, probability, and severity levels. Keep in mind that identified risks and their probability and impact can change throughout the project. This means that risks should be monitored for changes in their severity levels. This

TABLE 10.1

Risks with Impact, Probability, and Severity Levels (Single Period of Time)

Risk	Type	Impact (0–3)	Probability (0–3)	Severity = Impact × Probability
1. Java version compatibility	Technical	3	2	6
2. Inadequate resources	Operational	3	2	6
3. Scope changes	Schedule	3	2	6
4. Vendor dispute	Financial	2	1	2
5. Priority conflicts	Operational	2	1	2
				22

would be a basic function of risk management and oversight. The plan is to mitigate or eliminate the impact of risks from causing an impact on the project. The data from Table 10.1 are for a "single" period of time (i.e., one month), however, data should be created on a weekly or monthly basis to determine if risks are being monitored properly.

A way that risks can be tracked is by means of a risk Burndown Chart (Figure 10.1). The expectation is that risk severity levels should be getting lower (moving downwards on the graph) in terms of impact. Table 10.2 contains risk data for a four-month time frame and it shows impact, probability, and severity levels. Notice that the risk impact levels are decreasing (downward trend). This is what should be occurring under the proper risk management activities.

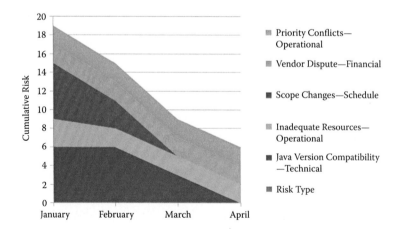

FIGURE 10.1
Risk Burndown Chart.

TABLE 10.2

Cumulative Risk Ratings for a Four-Month Time Period

Risk	Type	January Impact (0-3)	Prob. (0-3)	Severity = Impact × Prob.	February Impact (0-3)	Prob. (0-3)	Severity = Impact × Prob.	March Impact (0-3)	Prob. (0-3)	Severity = Impact × Prob.	April Impact (0-3)	Prob. (0-3)	Severity = Impact × Prob.
Java version compatibility	Technical	3	2	6	3	2	6	3	1	3	3	0	0
Inadequate resources	Operational	3	1	3	2	1	2	2	1	2	2	1	2
Scope changes	Schedule	3	2	6	3	1	3	3	0	0	3	0	0
Vendor dispute	Financial	2	1	2	2	1	2	2	1	2	2	1	2
Priority conflicts	Operational	2	1	2	2	1	2	2	1	2	2	1	2
				19			15			9			6

Figure 10.1 shows an example of a cumulative risk burndown graph based on the data from Table 10.2. The expectation is that the risk severity levels should be decreasing over a period of time. This would mean that risks are being proactively managed as required.

The author is under the distinct impression that many people believe that risk management is not a big component of agile methods. In actuality agile methods are in fact risk driven. We have already learned thus far that agile methods are value driven. We briefly touched on the fact that agile methods are risk driven as well. We now describe the risk-driven aspect of agility in more detail.

Iterations provide the opportunity to confront and mitigate high-risk items and to discover high-value opportunities on the agile project. As a result of transparency, potential or identified problems or opportunities are brought to the surface early and as a result, less time and money are spent on identifying actual risks. Work on the agile project is prioritized based on business priority and risk levels. Risky features get addressed as quickly as possible based on the return on investment (ROI) for each item in the backlog. Opportunities are addressed as changes that add value for the customer.

Let's get into greater detail as to how this is done. To begin, most projects are undertaken because of the ROI on the overall project. What we need to do is to divide the ROI across the product's overall feature list. For example, see Table 10.3 for a list of the prioritized product backlog and related ROI values.

Once we have determined the ROI per feature, we now need to calculate the expected monetary value (EMV) of each risk. According to the *PMBOK® Guide* (2013),* the EMV is a statistically based concept that

TABLE 10.3

Prioritized Product Backlog with ROI per Feature

Feature	Priority	ROI ($)
Works on the MAC	1	10,000
Works on Windows	1	8,000
Supports 5,000+ users	1	25,000
Java based	2	7,000
Citrix	2	4,000
Portable to the mainframe	3	3,000

---

* PMI (2013).

TABLE 10.4

Expected Monetary Value (EMV) Calculation

Feature	Priority	ROI ($)	Risk Impact ($) (How much does it cost to mitigate this risk?)	Risk Probability (%)	EMV ($) = Risk Impact ($) × Risk Probability (%)
Works on the MAC	1	10,000	5,000	75	3,750
Works on Windows	1	8,000	4,000	50	2,000
Supports 5,000+ users	1	25,000	20,000	45	9,000

determines average results of a future event that include a scenario that has a particular level of uncertainty. We observe the following when calculating EMV for risks and opportunities:

- EMV results for opportunities are positive values.
- EMV results for risks are negative values.
- When calculating the EMV for an entire project, the values of all possible outcomes are multiplied by the probability of occurrence and then adding the products of the values together. For example:
- Expected Monetary Value (EMV) = Risk Impact ($) × Risk Probability (%).

See Table 10.4 for an example of EMV calculations.

Once we have determined the EMV for the risks and the business value, we now have the item in the backlog rearranged and it is now referred to as a risk-adjusted backlog. See Table 10.5 for an example.

TABLE 10.5

Risk-Adjusted Backlog (Requirements and Risk Responses)

Prioritized Risks ($)	Prioritized Requirements Value (ROI; $)	Risk Adjusted Backlog ($)
Risk #1—9,000	Requirement #1—25,000	Requirement # 1—(25,000)
Risk #2—3,750	Requirement #2—10,000	Requirement #2—(10,000)
Risk #3—2,000	Requirement #3—8,000	Risk Action #1—(9,000)
		Requirement #3—(8,000)
		Risk #1—(3,750)
		Risk #3—(2,000)

MITIGATING RISKS WITH AGILE METHODS

Agile methods are known to inherently minimize risk. Following is a list of ways that risk mitigation occurs:

- The flexibility of agile methods automatically reduces risk in the business environment.
  - Risk is mitigated because agile methods are flexible with adding or changing user requirements at any time in the project. This provides the business a chance to respond to potential threats or opportunities from within the environment. Missing or forgotten requirements can be included as soon as they are identified. This results in low costs associated with managing this category of risks.
- Regular feedback reduces risk-related expectations.
  - As a result of the iterative nature of agile methods, there is adequate time to get feedback and establish expectations during the life cycle of the project. Stakeholders and the agile team are never caught with their pants down because of requirements that have been communicated inadequately.
- Agile team ownership supports reduced estimation risk.
  - When the agile team takes responsibility for estimates of backlog items, this leads to increased accuracy of the estimates that they provide which in turn results in the timely delivery of the product.
- Transparency is a risk reducer of undetected risk.
  - As a result of transparency, risks are always detected and addressed as early as possible. This leads to better risk management and mitigation. During daily meetings, obstacles are communicated on a regular basis.
- Iterative delivery causes a reduction in investment-related risk.
  - As value is being continuously delivered through the iterations, investment risk is automatically reduced for the end customer.

RISK MANAGEMENT FOR AGILE VERSUS TRADITIONAL PROJECT MANAGEMENT

With regard to traditional project management, a large amount of up-front planning occurs for identifying, evaluating, and developing risk response plans for project risks. When a new risk arises during project execution, it is added to the risk register and a risk owner is assigned to address the risk(s).

Agile methods (e.g., Scrum) are supportive of team members identifying risks and the Product Owner modifying the risk-adjusted prioritized backlog. This results in risks being constantly identified, added to the backlog, and prioritized along with other user stories. Risks are mitigated in the upcoming iteration (i.e., Sprint) and the agile team (Scrum team) has the responsibility for the management of the iteration (Sprint).

CHAPTER SUMMARY

In agile environments, risks are mitigated as a result of the project work being completed in iterations. There is a consistent outflow of product increments being developed in short development cycles. During these cycles, the product is being evaluated against expectations by all stakeholders (i.e., Product Owner, agile team, sponsor and agile leader). The risk management process on the agile project (e.g., Scrum) consists of the following steps:

1. *Identify risk:* This can be accomplished with risk checklists, brainstorming, risk breakdown structure, lessons learned from retrospect Sprints, and risk-based spikes.
2. *Assess risk:* The assessment is based upon probability and impact as we previously discussed in this chapter. This is also accomplished through risk meetings, probability trees, Pareto analysis, and so on. The author believes that project management professionals (PMPs) are already familiar with these tools and techniques. The expected monetary value (EVM) is also a way to assess risk and it has been discussed in this chapter.
3. *Prioritize risk:* This technique requires updating the prioritized product backlog with the identified risks.
   a. *Create a list of prioritized lists:* These risks can be prioritized by value by using the EVM technique.
   b. *Select the risks that can be mitigated:* This means that action should be planned and carried out by the agile team to mitigate (lessen) the impact of the risk.

    c. *Create a list of user stories in the backlog that have been prioritized based on value.*

    d. *Combine the lists from Steps b and c and prioritize by value* to get the updated risk-adjusted prioritized product backlog.

4. *Risk mitigation:* Agile methods have a built-in risk mitigation component. We will discuss this more in Chapter 16, "Agile Change Management."

5. *Risk communication:* A good method is to use a risk Burndown Chart (see Figure 10.1). Recall that if the agile project's risk management activities have been properly conducted, the Risk Burndown Chart should show a downward trend in the impact of all identified risks.

11

Agile People Skills

We now move to a discussion of people skills (soft skills), which is a critical component in successfully interacting with or managing others. It is important that leaders, management, developers, and stakeholders possess the ability to get along and work well with others in a team environment. From the author's perspective, the agile team needs to act professionally at all times and display a certain level of maturity. The agile project is team focused and must communicate on a face-to-face basis; the ability to negotiate effectively is mandatory. Following is an overview of several critical soft skills that are important on agile projects, particularly when engaging with stakeholders. The agile team (Product Owner, developers, and agile leader) must learn to use effective soft skills when dealing with others. (This list is not inclusive of all possible situations.)

- Listening to others
- Negotiating
- Addressing and resolving conflict
- Utilizing emotional intelligence
- Conducting effective meetings
- Embracing diversity
- Leading and managing effectively
- Embodying the PMI Code of Ethics

LISTENING

Proper listening refers to understanding what another person "means" rather than what that person has "said." The statement just made may not be clear to many, but words don't always get across the message as intended. Listening requires understanding what the person means because words can take on a variety of implications to different people. To gain a full understanding of what another person "means," it may be necessary to focus on body language in order to understand what is really being conveyed by the person who is speaking. Good listening requires an analysis as to how the words are being said and whether emphasis is being placed on specific syllables. The meaning of words can also be obtained based on whether the person is speaking publicly or privately as this is an indication of how important the message may be. Finally, it is important to understand we don't do our best listening when we are talking. It is a good idea to stop talking when we are trying to do our best job of listening.

NEGOTIATING

On traditional project management projects and from the author's experience, the project manager is responsible for the majority, if not all, of the negotiation activities. In contrast, the agile environment requires negotiation by all team members throughout the entire project. There is negotiation regarding what "done" should be, during the prioritization of the user stories, during the clarification of requirements, during costs discussions, and the list goes on and on. The customer and the agile team must negotiate often in order to reach a consensus on the velocity during iterations. There has to be a give and take approach (tradeoff) in order to reach an agreement during these negotiations or very little would ever get accomplished. The idea behind successful negotiations is that this activity needs to be pleasant and tradeoffs have to be made from all involved parties. The author believes that negotiation is as simple as making tradeoffs and nothing more.

ADDRESSING AND RESOLVING CONFLICT

Many of us have experienced conflict in the work environment on multiple occasions. It is almost a normal occurrence because of the different interests of stakeholders affected by projects. There is always a difference of opinion among people and this is indeed very normal. What is abnormal and a cause for concern are unhealthy interactions, angry individuals, and unresolved issues. This is the time when conflict needs to be addressed and resolved. Conflict is not always a negative situation. The goal is to use conflict in a positive way, specifically to engage stakeholders and resolve issues. The hope is that conflict can at times be resolved among the stakeholders before or after intervention by a neutral party. In the case of an intervention, facts need to be extracted from emotions. In the event that an intervention is unsuccessful, the parties can use a mediator (coach, manager, or agile leader) to get to the root of the conflict and offer suggestions for a resolution. There are situations where a win–lose decision has to be made in order to move forward and that would be a last resort option.

UTILIZING EMOTIONAL INTELLIGENCE

Agile team members must understand that it requires a certain degree of flexibility when dealing with uncertainty and unknown circumstances. It must be understood that in such situations, a healthy level of emotional intelligence, which is referred to as the capability to understand, evaluate, and affect the emotional well-being of others, including ourselves, is necessary. There are several facets to emotional intelligence:

- Self
  - Self-management
    - Self-control
    - Flexibility
    - Motivation and ambition
    - Carefulness
  - Self-awareness
    - Sureness in self
    - Emotional self-awareness
    - Correct self-assessment
- Others
  - Social skills
    - Self-control
    - Motivating leadership

- Developing other people
- Alliances and teamwork
• Social awareness
  - Compassion
  - Organizational consciousness
  - Understanding of surroundings

In other words, people need to understand themselves before they can understand others. From an emotional standpoint, we need to be in touch with our feelings and then evolve to controlling them. Each of us has the capability to control how we respond to external events. Once we understand that we do have control over how we react, we are improving our sense of self-awareness and improving our ability to manage ourselves. How we react to others has an enormous impact on the emotional health of the team. Team members should learn how to develop their own levels of social awareness and compassion for others. Specifically, a leader should be able to influence others in a positive way. The leader and agile team members may need to motivate, lead, and develop others and without emotional intelligence, leadership and teamwork have a high probability of being ineffective.

CONDUCTING EFFECTIVE MEETINGS

According to Griffiths (2012), conducting effective meetings is covered on the PMI-ACP exam and this knowledge area must be properly understood. We have discussed several types of agile meetings in Chapter 3 under the Scrum methodology. The exam refers to this topic as *Facilitation Methods*. In order to conduct effective meetings, the facilitator should focus on the following set of factors:[*]

• *Meeting Objectives:* What is the purpose of the meeting? Why are we having this meeting? What do we hope to accomplish? Objectives will keep the meeting on track.
• *Meeting Rules:* All participants should be made aware of the rules prior to the start of the meeting. The facilitator must enforce rules in order to meet objectives.

---

[*] Griffiths, M. (2012).

- *Meeting Time:* A timekeeper (preferably the facilitator) must keep the meeting within the scheduled time. The meeting duration should be established beforehand.
- *Meeting Assistance:* The facilitator should ensure that all participants are allowed to provide feedback. The focus should always be kept on the meeting objective and deviations should not be permitted.

EMBRACING DIVERSITY

Effective people skills include an awareness of diversity in the workplace. Cultural diversity is considered to be positive because it can result in a highly qualified team on the agile project. On the other hand, cultural differences can increase the complexity of communication discrepancies due to language differences. Most experienced IT professionals have worked on culturally diverse projects and are quite accustomed to different languages. There are also cases where team members may speak the same or similar language but there are apparent differences related to expressions, terminology, and culture. In any case, awareness is the first step toward embracing diversity. Once there is awareness, diversity differences can be addressed and resolved on a one-on-one or group basis simply by giving the affected party an opportunity to be understood.

LEADING AND MANAGING EFFECTIVELY

Agile methods value *"individuals and interactions over processes and tools."* A good leader must understand what motivates people in order to get their best attributes to the surface. In the fortunate event that personal and project goals line up, the end result is a win–win situation. There are distinct differences between leadership and management: the former focuses more on people and the latter focuses on the work. People need to be led and work needs to be managed. Those in a position of authority need to understand that both leadership and management skills are needed on projects.

In order to lead others effectively, there are certain characteristics that must be displayed in a leader. First, a leader must display honesty. In order to gain the trust of others, a leader must demonstrate a certain amount of trustworthiness from within. Any sign of deceit can quickly erode the trust of others. Once trust is lost, it is practically impossible to regain. Leaders should refrain from being dishonest in all situations and for all reasons.

A leader must also show a certain level of competence when leading others. If it is shown that a leader does not have a clue regarding technical matters and there is a pretense of such knowledge, then the leader's credibility can potentially be lost forever and the damage done is irreparable. In the event that the leader lacks specific technical knowledge, it is better to be humble and ask a team member for the needed information than to proceed as a fake.

Leaders must have the ability to motivate others toward the attainment of the project/product's vision. There may be times where team members may need a push to get them back on the right track. This is where the leader's skill in motivating others comes into play. Keeping the morale up high on projects is also a critical skill that leaders should have.

According to Griffiths (2012), there are 12 principles for leading the agile project that have been established by Jeffrey Pinto in his book, *Project Leadership: From Theory to Practice*:

1. Identify the needs of the project team.
2. Understand the project's requirements.
3. Function for the best interests of the team and project.
4. Establish an environment for functional accountability.
5. Develop a vision for the finished product.
6. Apply the vision to model your own behavior as leader.
7. Be the central figure in successful project team development.
8. Acknowledge team conflict as positive.
9. Manage with a focus on ethical behavior.
10. Include ethics as an integral part of your thinking as a leader.
11. Reflect on the project.
12. Think in reverse.

The author believes that the best leader is one who does not noticeably interfere but allows the team to function in such a manner that at the end of a project, the team will look up and say, "We did it together!" This is the pinnacle of good leadership.

TABLE 11.1

Team Formation versus Situational Leadership

Team Formation Stages	Situational Leadership Stages
(1) Forming	(1) Supporting
(2) Storming	(2) Delegating
(3) Norming	(3) Directing
(4) Performing	(4) Coaching
(5) Adjourning or mourning	n/a

Adaptive Leadership[*]

This type of leadership is defined as being adaptable when determining the manner in which to lead others based on certain conditions and team characteristics. Another term for adaptive leadership is referred to as *situational leadership*. In the case of traditional project management, the leader would need to work with the team through the normal stages of team development [(1) forming, (2) storming, (3) norming, (4) performing and optionally (5) adjourning or mourning]. For agile projects, the recommendation is to use a more "performance-based" approach where it is envisioned that the project can get more out of the team. This is referred to as Situational Leadership and it includes the following stages: (1) supporting, (2) delegating, (3) directing, and (4) coaching. See Table 11.1 for a visual comparison of team formation and situational leadership stages.

Servant Leadership

We now discuss a specific type of leadership for the agile environment, referred to as servant leadership. What is servant leadership? This type of leadership understands that the agile team is responsible for getting work done on the project, which results in the achievement of the business value. The leader (agile project manager or ScrumMaster, e.g.) is required to focus on removing obstacles from the team's path so that work can get completed. The servant leader is responsible for:

- Preventing others from unnecessarily interrupting the team so that work can be done.
  - Many of us have experienced the business side of the project making requests or changes that are not a part of the agreed-upon

[*] Griffiths, M. (2012).

scope. To prevent these types of interruptions, the ScrumMaster or agile project manager must keep the team away from interruptions by all means possible. Colocation is one idea that can keep interferences at a minimum.

- Removing hindrances that interfere with obtaining progress.
  - During the daily standup meetings, the team has 15 minutes to discuss what has been completed, what is going to be completed, and to describe any obstacles. The ScrumMaster, for example, is required to document these obstacles and take steps to remove these impediments as quickly as possible.
- Reiterating the project's vision.
  - The vision (project goal) must be repeated as often as possible because it is extremely important to the success of the team in order to keep the focus. The team must work in the same direction with the same vision and must not stray in order to experience success. Divergences are not allowed and focusing on the vision is a good way to keep the team on track.
- Providing food and water.
  - This is really not about providing food and water; this is just a way to describe providing for the team so that they are content in terms of being fed, happy, and productive. Whatever is determined to motivate the team, the leader should make every attempt to provide incentives to keep the team engaged.

According to SCRUMstudy (2013), Robert K. Greenleaf introduced the concept of servant leadership in his essay, *The Servant as Leader.* As a servant leader, the first priority is to serve. The next choice for the servant leader is the natural aspiration to lead others. This role is not the same as a person who wants to lead others first and serve others second. The leader-first and servant-first roles fall into very dissimilar categories. The servant-first role desires to take care of and serve others and the leader-first role has the desire to lead first rather than serve. Servant leaders share their authority with others as they listen with compassion and understanding. Desired results are achieved by the servant leaders (ScrumMaster and Product Owner, e.g.) by attending to the needs of the team. The servant leader is concerned with the positive effects of his or her servitude to others. To clarify, the Product Owner is also a servant leader to the team.

---

* Greenleaf, R.K. (1991, 2008)

Aside from good listening skills and showing empathy for others, the servant leader needs to possess a host of necessary personality traits. The responsibility of this role in serving others is not to be taken lightly. The person in this role must understand how to use persuasion to gain agreement among the agile team. In the servant role, authority is rarely if ever used to influence the team. These leaders are also very committed to the development of others in the company. It is not uncommon for this role to take on the responsibility of cultivating and coaching other workers. Having a mature and instinctual mind-set also permits this role to rebuild and strengthen relationships as well as function as a sounding board for others when needed. The capability to apply lessons learned from past situations and to predict outcomes of decisions and circumstances is also a desired trait of the servant leader. Finally, this type of leader must be ethical (as should all types of leaders). The possession of a strong sense of awareness is important in understanding values, ethics, and the proper use of power.

EMBODYING THE PMI CODE OF ETHICS

The PMI has established a code of ethics and professional behavior as it pertains to relationships with others on agile projects.* The four main areas are responsibility, respect, fairness, and honesty. Those who are project management professionals (PMPs) or PMs in general are already aware of how important ethical behavior is on projects and during interactions with stakeholders. The code of ethics boils down to:

- Be responsible.
  - Make decisions based on what is best for the company.
  - Protect proprietary information.
  - Report unethical behavior and violations.
- Show respect.
  - Be cooperative.
  - Respect cultural differences.
  - Show good faith when negotiating.
  - Don't avoid conflict; deal with it head-on.
  - Don't use your position to manipulate others.

---

* PMI. (2013).

- Be fair.
  - Don't accept bribery and do act impartially.
  - Be aware and fully disclose conflicts of interests.
  - No discrimination.
  - Don't use your position for personal gain.
- Be honest.
  - Understand the truth.
  - Tell the truth in all communications.

CHAPTER SUMMARY

Agile methods acknowledge that projects are undertaken by people and that they are more important than processes. Soft skills can be described as emotional intelligence, which we have covered in this chapter. Individual soft skills are collectively important in teams and businesses as a whole. Basically, soft skills boil down to personality, communication, language, and other characteristics that define how we deal with others. Feelings, insights, and emotions are also important soft skills that play a role in interactions with other people. In today's world, soft skills are equally important as hard (technical) skills. We must remember to place the proper level of importance on our relationships with others at all times. The message is "Treat each other well!"

12

Agile Teams

The agile team must be self-organized and self-directed. This means that the team members are empowered to determine how best to perform their jobs based upon their experience and skill levels. Agile methods are based on the belief that individuals are the ones who actually perform the work and are therefore best suited to determine the order and manner in which the work should be performed. When people are given the opportunity to self-organize and plan their own work, the end result is an invested team that functions under a servant-leadership methodology as we discussed in Chapter 11. The project manager's role (or leadership role such as a ScrumMaster, e.g.) protects the team from disruptions, removes obstacles, provides support, and reiterates the vision on a regular basis. In addition, as teams become more experienced, they become self-directing, developing their own rules and making their own technical decisions.*

The agile team is also referred to as the *"Define/Build/Test Team."†* This definition is based on the agile team's responsibilities:

- Define.
  - Elicit and prioritize the requirements.
  - Design the product.
- Build.
  - Write the code.
  - Write the tests.
  - Implement the product.
- Test.
  - Execute the tests for the solution.
  - Validate the product against the user stories.

---

* Griffiths, M. (2012).
† Leffingwell, LLC. (2014).

The agile team must build, define, and test product increments of customer value within a short period of time in addition to sharing the responsibility of delivering a product of value. On the other hand, the traditional project manager is professed to hold 100% of the responsibility for the outcome of the project. As previously mentioned, the agile team is typically small with an average team size of six to ten members. A known benefit of a small team is the fact that people have the opportunity to experience heightened interactions with each other. Recall from Chapter 6 that face-to-face communications have the highest level of effectiveness in comparison with other methods. We now move our discussion to a detailed analysis of the agile team and its unique characteristics when compared to the traditional project management team.

AGILE TEAM CHARACTERISTICS

One important attribute of the agile team is its cross-functional members. What do we really mean by this term? Simply put, this refers to a team that has all of the necessary skills to deliver value to the customer. On traditional project management teams, each member is assigned to one functional area (development, technical writing, etc.). However, on the agile cross-functional team, a single member may be skilled in more than one functional area (testing, development, databases, etc.). The traditional project team will have all of the necessary functional talent but the team size might be large, whereas the agile team is always going to be small in size. There is rarely a need to seek knowledge outside the cross-functional agile team. The work on the agile team is given directly to members and not from leader to team in the traditional sense. Table 12.1 shows a general comparison of the agile team with the traditional project team.

The traditional project management team has a tiered management approach with the project manager having full authority to delegate tasks downward to the project team. Each team member is held accountable for his or her assignments rather than the whole group sharing responsibility for the outcome. In the case where a team member does not accomplish what the project manager has asked of him, then this is viewed as a potential problem. The project manager is responsible for the success of the project because he or she makes all of the decisions on the project alone. The agile team as a whole does not take direction or instruction

TABLE 12.1

Agile Team versus Traditional Team

Agile Team	Traditional Team
Self-organized	Leader-organized
Self-directed	Leader-directed
Cross-functional	Functional
All team members held accountable	Project manager held accountable
Servant leadership	Direct and regulate leadership
Small teams only	Large teams
Multiskilled team members	Single-skilled team members
Generalizing specialists	Specialists
Make their own decisions	Leader makes decisions for the team
Focus on group success	Focus on individual success

from anyone. This type of team manages and directs itself. The entire team has to be in agreement with decisions made and as a result, the team is highly effective and harmonious.

The agile team's structure is very different from the traditional on-your-own–based information technology (IT) project. To clarify, *on-your-own* means that the project manager alone is responsible for the project. In contrast, on the agile project, the team is collectively responsible and the role of the project manager is shared by the Product Owner, development team, and agile leader. Value is delivered throughout the project, totally unlike that of the typical IT project. There are no physically separate departments that have specific functions because agile projects have cross-functional team members who are capable of performing all needed work tasks within the teams.

AGILE TEAM MAGIC

So how does the agile team accomplish all that has to be done within short, specific time-boxes? Do they use some sort of magic? Some may perceive the feats of the agile team to be magical. How is it done? The answer is the three Cs.

- Collaboration
- Communication
- Commitment

Collaboration

Remember the agile value from Chapter 2, "*Customer collaboration over contract negotiation*"? In addition to collaborating with the customer, the agile team must join forces with each other in order to meet project goals as described in the project vision statement.* There are, in fact, several tactics that need to be implemented during the collaboration process. The team must be fully aware of what others on the team are undertaking so that it can use each other's contributions to develop the product. The team must then divide the work up and distribute it among the members and then put it all back together again once the individual work components have been completed. In addition, the team must be versed in implementing technology in incredible and unimaginable ways. This is where we can say the real magic occurs on the agile team.

During the requirements clarification process on the agile project, collaboration occurs between the Product Owner and team to clarify the work that needs to be completed based on the user stories. There is consistent collaboration between the stakeholders (i.e., executive team, sponsor, managers, agile project team, users, and support groups) and the Product Owner so that a prioritized product backlog can be used to develop the product and related deliverables. As a result of collaboration, the amount of rework and the volume of requests to make changes are limited.

Collaboration is also used for risk identification and analysis. During the team meetings, for example, potential risks are identified, evaluated, and risk responses realized. Meetings are the collaboration events that provide the team opportunities for continuous improvement on a regular basis. Discussions during collaboration provide clarity and opportunities for the team to understand each other's strengths (and weaknesses as well). In the case of a team member experiencing technical difficulty, other members are made aware of the need to provide assistance so that there are no interruptions during the iterations. Recall that lessons learned are conducted throughout the iterations. This is another chance to collaborate and make improvements to processes and practices during the project rather than waiting until the end.

---

* SCRUMstudy. (2013).

Collaborative Agile Games

The agile team uses games to collaborate with each other. This is done so that all stakeholders have the same understanding and are in agreement with the proposed solution for the product. The games are referred to as collaborative games. A discussion of the various types of games follows:

- Start Your Day[*]
  - The objective of this game is to gain understanding of when and how a product is used by the customer.
  - By focusing on when a product is used, a seller can gain better awareness of how the product is used.
  - The game is played by asking the customer to define the events that pertain to their usage of the product. This information should be written down on paper based on daily, weekly, monthly, and annual time frames. As the customer is generating this information, the seller should be alerted to factors as to how the product helps or hinders the customer.
  - This game is effective because as the customer provides the "when" of using the product, the ability to understand the "how" is improved so that the product can be made better.
- Product Box[†]
  - The objective of this game is to identify a product's most sensational features.
  - This game begins by asking the customer to design a product box for the item up for sale. The product box must be the one that the customer wants to purchase. During this process, what the customer believes is important is revealed.
  - The customer should also be asked to develop a slogan for the product that is appealing to him or her. The game is completed by asking the customer to sell the product to the creator of the item.
  - As the customer is pretending to sell the item, real problems that the customer wants to solve with the product are revealed. This game gives the customers an opportunity to reveal and express their needs as they pretend to sell the product themselves.

---

[*] Innovation Games. (2013c).
[†] Innovation Games. (2013b).

- Me and My Shadow[*]
  - The objective of this game is to identify the customer's undisclosed needs.
  - This game is designed to reveal how a product can be used in nontraditional ways.
  - The creator of the product should observe the customer using the product or service so that information can be obtained as to how it is used that may appear to be different than expected.
  - This game is effective because it is a research technique that provides insight into different ways that customers might use a product.

Communication

We know that the agile team communicates face to face with each other and this is another reason why they are able to be so effective. The team must communicate on a consistent basis with all stakeholders to make certain that everyone has the same understanding of the project requirements and goals. In addition to face-to-face communications, there are other ways to provide information such as, for example, graphs and charts displayed in the team's work area. The term *information radiator* was created by Alistar Cockburn[†] and it is used to describe information that is made public to the project stakeholders in highly visible locations. Information is "radiated" about the project in a highly transparent manner. An example of statistics that are commonly displayed on information radiators includes but is not limited to the following:

- Task assignments
- Defect data
- Team velocity
- Burnup/Burndown Charts
- Risks
- Retrospective data
- Product features

---

[*] Innovation Games. (2013a).
[†] Griffiths, M. (2012).

Commitment

The agile team commits to the work they can complete within a specified time box of two weeks to one month, with a preference for the shorter time frame. The team has the authority to estimate the work they can do per iteration as well as deciding upon the entire technical result for the product. In addition, the team is responsible for delivering a quality product to the customer as they continuously determine ways to strengthen and improve the capability of the group. Decisions are made quickly and frequently because of colocation. There has to be a certain level of trust on the agile team. The completion of the work is driven by the team sharing the same goals and getting consistent feedback with regard to the product. Respect has to be given to each other in order to complete the work in the allotted iteration time frame because there is no time to be wasted. The mission of the team is to deliver value to the customer. There has to be a certain level of commitment in order to reach these goals.

AGILE TEAM SIZE

The agile team size is typically small (less than or equal to 10 members), however, agile project management can be used on large projects as well. In the case of a team size greater than 10, it then becomes necessary to implement the project with multiple agile teams. In this circumstance, the teams are working toward a common goal and must coordinate with each other on a regular basis. The leadership role for multiple agile teams is referred to as (in the case of Scrum, e.g.) the Scrum of Scrums or Scrum of Scrum of Scrums depending upon the team structure. Figure 12.1 shows an example of the hierarchy of this role.

MOTIVATING THE AGILE TEAM

There are different things that motivate people on the job. Some want a higher-level position; others want an increased level of compensation. There are also others who value flexible time or working remotely as much

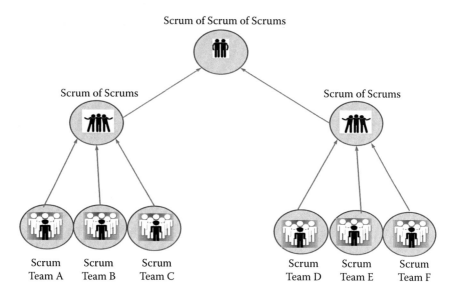

FIGURE 12.1
Scrum of Scrum of Scrums.

as possible. It is important on the agile team (or any team for that matter) that the motivation level is consistently high. What exactly is team motivation? The author believes that it is a way to encourage team members to give 130% effortlessly on a consistent basis. That number may be a slight overkill, however, a number equal to 100% is the minimum performance expectation and anything larger is a delightful bonus. On the agile project, the team must be motivated enough to show enthusiasm in reaching the project's goals. Individual personal goals don't mix very well on the agile project because of the time-boxes, the fast pace, and the push to deliver value to the customer consistently. The software must be working and the customer must be satisfied. The servant leader (ScrumMaster or the Product Owner) must take on the role of a motivator who is able to align the goals of the team members with those of the project. This will result in a successful product delivery.

ALIGNING THE AGILE TEAM

Getting the agile team aligned with project goals requires a detailed understanding of the factors that motivate each individual and the group as a whole. Once this information is discovered, these fundamentals can be included in the overall project. The objectives of the team can be intertwined with the project goals resulting in increased motivation and greater productivity levels. This may sound like a stretch, however, these actions are actually effective. For example, giving team members authority to lead others in specific areas that they have expressed interest in is a good way to mix personal and project goals. These types of alignment activities should occur throughout the project, either on an iteration basis or during meetings when everyone is present. On the other hand, team recognition events can be used as an effective technique to boost morale and motivation levels.

COACHING THE AGILE TEAM

Analogous to aligning project and personal goals, coaching should be done at both the individual and group levels. The idea behind coaching is to engage in a discussion that is truthful, courteous, and helpful. Coaching is not about criticizing and reprimanding others. With one-on-one coaching, the idea is to guide the person gently and allow him (or let him believe) that the idea being conveyed is his own. The coach should always give assurance that the information being discussed is confidential and won't be shared with others.

PROBLEM RESOLUTION

It is no secret that the approach a team uses to recognize and resolve problems will have a massive impact on the success or failure of a project. Many of us know from everyday living that problems don't go away on their own accord; they have to be addressed and resolved. The same is true for problems on a project, whether it be agile or traditional. Unresolved problems can result in rework, budget overages, and schedule slippages. Problems need to be uncovered and corrected with no exceptions. As many of us have learned with defective software, it is better to find the defect early rather than later. The costs to correct defects are significantly much greater when found later in the project. The earlier the detection of problems, the better.

PROBLEM DETECTION

The daily standup meeting is the ideal time for problem detection on the agile project. During these time-boxed meetings, team members are given the opportunity to describe any obstacles they are facing. This provides for quick identification and early resolution of problems. We now begin our discussion of several additional techniques that can be used on the agile project to detect problems.

Cycle Time

According to Griffiths (2012), *cycle time* is a technique used to determine the length of time it takes to complete a task. Basically, the start and finish times are recorded in order to capture the duration. From Chapter 7, recall that work in progress (WIP) should be limited because it represents money that is invested but has no return on the investment. A bottleneck in the system has the potential to be hidden behind WIP. In addition, there is a high risk of costly rework because the deliverable has not yet been accepted by the customer. These are reasons why WIP must be limited. We can use cycle time as a way to keep an eye on WIP. Long cycle times can result in bigger volumes of WIP. We calculate cycle time as:

$$\text{Cycle Time} = \text{WIP}/\text{Throughput}$$

- The *cycle time* is the beginning and ending times for the completion of the work. The project's cycle time is the average for all of the work items on the project.
- The level of *WIP* is a key indicator of how much work we have pending. This is also an indicator of holdups and rework risks.
- *Throughput* is the amount of "productivity" from a particular procedure (the amount of work that the agile team can accomplish).

We now use the formula in real-world situations to show how cycle time is used. Once we have determined the cycle time of how long work takes to be completed, this information can be used to detect problems.

- A television manufacturer makes 200 flat screen TVs a day. The average number of these types of TVs that are in production is 2,000. We need to determine the cycle time, which is the average time it takes to produce a TV.
  - Cycle time = 2,000/200 = 10
  - It takes 10 days to finish production of a flat screen TV
- For the problem above, if the cycle time is 5 days and the WIP is 500, then what is throughput?
  - Throughput = WIP/cycle time
  - Throughput = 500/5 = 100
  - The manufacturer makes 100 TVs per day
- What is the change in the throughput from the problem above in terms of percentage?
  - The change is from 200 to 100 in throughput
  - 200 – 100 = 100 (the differences between the throughput)
  - 100/200 = .50 or 50%

Quality

When we think of problems and their resolutions, we think of quality management. What exactly is quality? The author believes that quality is meeting or exceeding the requirements, delighting the customer, and so on. Quality means different things to different people but the bottom line is the person paying for the product or service must be satisfied. According to the PMI (2013), quality management is: "The processes and activities of the performing organization that determine the quality policies; objectives, and responsibilities in order for the project to satisfy the needs for which it was undertaken."[*] We will now discuss ways that quality is achieved on the agile project.

V & V

Verification and validation (V&V) is another technique used to detect and resolve problems. This activity is done on a rather frequent basis and its purpose is to make sure that everything is proceeding as expected. For the agile project, V&V activities are conducted as follows:

---

[*] PMI. (2013).

- Continuous integration
  - Verifies that code integration is error free.
- Unit testing
  - Executed every few minutes by developers to verify that the functionality works correctly; verifies that the code produces the desired outcome.
- Customer collaboration
  - Occurs frequently so that feedback is provided on design and other project objectives.
- Standup meeting
  - Validates task assignments and completions, issues, and obstacles.
- Acceptance testing
  - Verifies that requirements are accepted by the customer.
- Iteration demonstration
  - Verifies that an iteration is successful.

Continuous Integration

In the agile realm, continuous integration is a technique that is frequently used to integrate new (or modified) code with the existing code. This is a way for the team to address problems as soon as possible. This is also a way to lessen the risk of integration problems that could occur if too many people attempt to make changes that don't incorporate well. A continuous integration system has the following components:

- *Source code control:* Version control for the build files.
- *Build tools:* Source code compiler.
- *Test tools:* During the build process, functional unit tests will need to be executed to ensure that the software works.
- *Triggered scheduler:* Capability to implement builds based on a set schedule.
- *Notifications:* Capability to provide notifications (pass or failure status).

Problem Solving

What is the best way to solve problems on the agile project? There are always going to be problems to be solved on every project, whether it is agile or traditional. On the traditional project, the project manager is mainly responsible for problem solving (or at least it appears that way to many). The agile project is different because the entire team is responsible for detecting, analyzing, and resolving problems that occur. Problem solving by the agile team is carried out in three distinct steps:

1. Collect information.
   a. This is done so that the entire team shares a similar perception of the identified problem. Data are used so the team can focus on facts and avoid speculation. There are multiple techniques for this process, however, the team is free to decide on the approach that works well for them as a whole.
2. Create acumen.
   a. This is the process of the team collaborating with each other in order to make some sense of the problem. The data should be analyzed from the previous step in order to make a determination as to the allegations. Brainstorming is a good technique to use during this process, however, the team again is free to decide upon the approach.
3. Determine actions.
   a. The final step is to make a decision(s) as to what needs to be done to solve the problem at hand. Actions that need to be taken need to be decided upon by the team. Experiments should be conducted that validate the proposed approach and goals should be set to track progress and resolution of the problem.

CHAPTER SUMMARY

The team should only be asked to participate in problem solving when the solution is moderately complex or when there are no obviously known remedies that currently exist. The project team is a good resource to use for problem solving on the agile project. In many cases, the team is best qualified for problem identification, analysis, and resolution because they are often the ones closest to the problems that occur on projects. Often the best ideas come from the workers and the agile team is no exception to this rule. The agile team is self-directed and self-managed so it is only natural to utilize their expertise collectively. Even though the team would more than likely be very eager to engage in problem resolution, caution must be made not to involve them in petty matters that are unwarranted. The team's involvement should be used for "genuine" problems and not those that are considered mundane and insignificant.

13

Agile Certifications

This chapter is an identification of the agile certifications that are currently in existence as of 2014. What does it really mean to be certified in agile methodologies? That question depends upon which type of certification is being evaluated. The agile certifications listed in Table 13.1 are discussed in this chapter.

PROJECT MANAGEMENT INSTITUTE AGILE CERTIFIED PRACTITIONER (PMI-ACP)

The Project Management Institute's Agile Certified Practitioner[*] is a global credential that identifies a professional-level knowledge of agile concepts, practices, tools, and techniques across diverse agile methodologies. When the credential is earned, a potential employer knows that the holder has attained a professional level of competence in agile methods. The PMI is a highly credible organization that certifies individuals in project management practices. Benefits of this certification include increased professional resourcefulness in project management and the attainment of a credential from an organization that is highly respected all over the world. The PMI-ACP credential is maintained by earning 30 professional development units (PDUs) in agile project management for each three-year cycle after attainment. PMI's Continuing Certification Requirements (CCR) online program is used to report PDU information. Table 13.2 outlines the eligibility requirements for the PMI-ACP credential.

---

[*] PMI. 2014.

TABLE 13.1

Agile Certifications

Certification	Acronym	Organization
Agile Certified Practitioner	PMI-ACP	Project Management Institute (PMI)
Certified ScrumMaster	CSM	Scrum Alliance
Certified Scrum Coach	CSC	Scrum Alliance
Certified Scrum Product Owner	CSPO	Scrum Alliance
Certified Scrum Developer	CSD	Scrum Alliance
Certified Scrum Professional	CSP	Scrum Alliance
Certified Scrum Trainer	CST	Scrum Alliance
Scrum Developer Certified	SDC	SCRUMstudy
ScrumMaster Certified	SMC	SCRUMstudy
Agile Expert Certified	AEC	SCRUMstudy
Scrum Product Owner Certified	SPOC	SCRUMstudy
Expert ScrumMaster	ESM	SCRUMstudy
Scrum Certified Trainer	SCT	SCRUMstudy

TABLE 13.2

PMI-ACP Eligibility Requirements

Requirement	Description
General project experience	2,000 hours working on project teams within the last five years (An active PMP® or PgMP® will satisfy this requirement.)
Agile project experience	1,500 hours working on agile project teams or with agile methodologies and these hours are in addition to the 2,000 hours required in "general project experience" above. These hours must be earned within the last three years.
Training in agile practices	21 contact hours that must be earned in agile practices.
Educational background	Secondary degree (high school diploma, associate's degree, or global equivalent).
Examination	Tests knowledge of agile fundamentals.

Source: Derived from PMI, 2014

SCRUM ALLIANCE CERTIFIED SCRUMMASTER (CSM)*

The Scrum Alliance was created to change the manner in which complex projects are undertaken. Scrum is an agile development methodology

---

* Scrum Alliance. (2014a).

TABLE 13.3

Eligibility Requirements for the Certified ScrumMaster (CSM) Credential

Requirement	Description
Certified ScrumMaster certificate	In order to earn the certificate, a person is required to take a two-day CSM course from a Certified Scrum trainer. Progress must be shown through the online CSM test.
CSM test	Only after completing the CSM course is the candidate eligible to take the CSM test. A passing score requires at least 24 out of 35 questions to be answered correctly.
Acceptance of the license agreement	This is done once the CSM test has been successfully completed.
Completion of the Scrum Alliance membership profile	The CSM must become a member of Scrum Alliance after passing the test.

used across the globe. The Scrum Alliance offers the ScrumMaster certification which indicates that the credential holder has a thorough understanding of the Scrum framework. As we discussed in Chapter 3, the ScrumMaster's role coaches the team in the use of Scrum principles. This role has a strong understanding in the practice of Scrum, including roles, activities, and artifacts. In addition, this is a servant leader role that helps the team understand the Scrum methodology, protects the team from both internal and external distractions, and removes obstacles so that the team works harmoniously together. The credential offers additional benefits such as access to user groups and social networks, and specific remunerations that are only available for Scrum Alliance's members. A CSM is also given a profile page and permission to use a logo that highlights his or her credential on the organization's website. Table 13.3 lists the requirements for the ScrumMaster certification.

After the CSM credential is obtained, Scrum concepts and practices need to be improved upon consistently with a personal commitment to continuous improvement. This requires an investment in increasing knowledge and skills in Scrum and agile concepts. The alliance recommends the following activities as ways to remain committed:

- Join user group(s).
- Contribute to an article on the Scrum Alliance website.
- Participate in Scrum Alliance events.
- Aspire to become a Certified Scrum Professional (CSP) as a next step upward.

- Join the Scrum Alliance group on LinkedIn.
- Maintain a profile on the Scrum Alliance website.

The activities listed above are applicable to all Scrum Alliance credentials.

SCRUM ALLIANCE CERTIFIED SCRUM COACH (CSC)[*]

The Scrum Alliance's Certified Scrum Coach (CSC) is considered to be an expert in the Scrum framework. These professionals have hands-on experience and are well versed in Scrum doctrines and practices. This role is responsible for providing guidance to organizations that need assistance with the challenges associated with Scrum implementation. Generally speaking, this credential holder is experienced in assisting multiple organizations with the use of Scrum. The CSC has experience with numerous Scrum teams, products, project phases, situations, or skills. This role helps teams understand how to increase their collaboration activities and performance levels that are required for Scrum. The implementation of Scrum is considered to be an organizational change that simply does not happen overnight. The CSC role assists the Scrum team and management with removing obstacles during the transformation process so that Scrum can be successfully embraced as planned. Even though Scrum may appear to be simple to some, the CSC role fully understands that implementation requires a change in one's mindset and the need to attain progressive skills. There are many companies that need assistance during the navigation of the process to become agile. This CSC role is most needed to advise top leaders and organizations as a whole, to engage in stakeholder discussions, and to lead the way to becoming agile by challenging the existing state of affairs. Table 13.4 outlines a list of requirements for the attainment of the CSC credential.

SCRUM ALLIANCE CERTIFIED SCRUM PRODUCT OWNER (CSPO)[†]

The Certified Scrum Product Owner is well versed in Scrum terminology, practices, and principles. This role is generally the closest to the business

---

[*] Scrum Alliance. (2014b).
[†] Scrum Alliance. (2014c).

TABLE 13.4

Scrum Alliance Certified Scrum Coach (CSC) Eligibility Requirements

Requirement	Description
Have a current Scrum credential	Must already be a Certified Scrum Professional (CSP)
1,500 hours of Scrum coaching over the past five years	Demonstrate this requirement based on a comprehensive application
Experience in coaching Scrum	Have coaching experience across multiple teams and/or organizations
Client references	Provide two different client references that verify coaching experience and skills
Active engagement and contribution in Scrum	Be able to demonstrate engagement and contribution to the Scrum community over the past three years

TABLE 13.5

Scrum Alliance Certified Scrum Product Owner (CSPO) Eligibility Requirements

Requirements	Description
Complete a two-day course	CSPO course taught by a Certified Scrum Trainer
Understand specific Scrum terminology	Topics include but are not limited to: • Stakeholder management • Return on investment (ROI) • Backlog grooming • User story creation • Acceptance criteria for user stories • Definition of "done"

side of the Scrum project. The CSPO is given the authority by the organization that he or she represents to get the product delivered along with satisfying all stakeholders, which is not always an easy task. In addition, as we have discussed in prior chapters, this role is responsible for maintenance of the prioritized product backlog. Table 13.5 outlines the eligibility requirements for the CSPO credential.

The benefits associated with the CSPO credential include:

- Capability to fulfill the role of Product Owner on the Scrum team
- Access to user group(s), social networks, and additional exclusive resources for CSPOs
- Receive a profile page on the Scrum Alliance's website with a special logo used to highlight the credential

SCRUM ALLIANCE CERTIFIED SCRUM DEVELOPER (CSD)*

The Certified Scrum Developer (CSD) is able to demonstrate that he or she has completed formalized training and has the technical skills necessary to understand Scrum principles and specialized agile engineering concepts. This credential sets the holder apart from others in the field because it illustrates a commitment to continuous improvement and it helps with becoming an improved practitioner of Scrum. Table 13.6 outlines the eligibility requirements for the credential.

TABLE 13.6

Scrum Alliance Certified Scrum Developer (CSD) Eligibility Requirements

Requirements	Description
Formal training	Minimum of five days of formal training taught by Scrum Alliance Registered Education Provider (REP).
Formal training	At least three days must be technical training through CSD technical skills course.
Formal training	At least one day must be devoted to studying and completing Scrum through an Introduction to Scrum course or a Certified ScrumMaster (CSM) course.
Formal training	For days four and five, complete either a Certified ScrumMaster certification or attend a one-day Scrum elective course and a one-day introduction to Scrum course.
	The applicant must be able to demonstrate an understanding of Agile engineering practices by passing a CSD assessment/evaluation provided by the REP/trainer.
	The REP/trainer uploads and pays the certification fees for students as they take CSD track courses in 2014.
CSD Certification requirements for 2014 (Scrum Alliance Member):	Scrum Alliance members and a CSM must take a three-day CSD-track technical course, then will receive notification to accept the CSD license, and the CSD certification will be added to the member's profile.
	There is no need to apply. The certification is good for two years.
CSD Certification requirements for 2014 (Not a Scrum Alliance Member yet):	Not yet a Scrum Alliance member at the time of the first CSD track course, then candidate will receive membership for one year.
	After completion of all CSD requirements, as listed above, candidate will receive CSD certification notification. The certification is good for two years.
Application submitted prior to 2014:	Submit an application and a $150 certification payment to secure active CSD status for two years.

---

* Scrum Alliance. (2014d).

TABLE 13.7

Scrum Alliance Certified Scrum Professional (CSP) Eligibility Requirements

Requirements	Description
Active credential holder	Either CSM, CSPO, or CSD
Agile/Scrum work experience gained within the past 5 years	Minimum 36 months implementing Scrum inside organizations as a team member, Product Owner, or ScrumMaster
Scrum Education Units (SEUs) from past three years	• CSM (up to 16 SEUs) • CSD (up to 24 SEUs) • and/or CSPO (up to 16 SEUs)

SCRUM ALLIANCE CERTIFIED SCRUM PROFESSIONAL (CSP)*

The Certified Scrum Professional is experienced, trained, and knowledgeable in the practices of Scrum. This role challenges Scrum teams to improve their implementation of Scrum and other agile methods. This credential demonstrates that the holder is an advanced and experienced Scrum practitioner who has gone the extra mile by being dedicated to continuous improvement. Table 13.7 outlines the eligibility requirements for the CSP credential.

SCRUM ALLIANCE CERTIFIED SCRUM TRAINER (CST)†

The Certified Scrum Trainer is licensed to teach only those courses for which she holds a credential and for which she has provided training materials. This role trains others on the principles and values contained within the Scrum foundation. The CST is qualified to assist organizations and individuals in adopting the agile framework and providing guidance on how to exploit the benefits. Table 13.8 provides the list of eligibility requirements.

---

* Scrum Alliance (2014e).
† Scrum Alliance. (2014f).

TABLE 13.8

Scrum Alliance Certified Scrum Trainer (CST) Eligibility Requirements

Requirements	Description
Existing credential holder	CSP in good standing
Submit CST application	Provide proof of cotraining with application
	Provide references from current Scrum Alliance reviews of the application package
Trainer Approval Community (TAC) reviews of application	Applicant needs four or five members to approve the application
In-person interview for accepted applicants	Attendance at Global Scrum Gathering where five to seven members are required to approve the application
Approved applicants	Attainment of CST
Declined applicants	Feedback provided to declined applicants along with encouragement to reapply
Application Fee	$250

SCRUMSTUDY SCRUM DEVELOPER CERTIFIED (SDC)*

The Scrum Developer Certified credential is considered to be entry level and is designed for team members and others who interact with any Scrum team. The purpose of this certification is to enable Scrum team members to know just enough about Scrum so they can effectively make contributions to a Scrum project. Table 13.9 outlines the requirements for the attainment of the SDC credential.

TABLE 13.9

SCRUMstudy Scrum Developer Certified (SDC) Eligibility Requirements

Requirements	Description
Education	None
Experience	None
Eligibility criteria	Anyone on a Scrum team or anyone who interacts with any Scrum team

---

* SCRUMstudy. (2014a).

TABLE 13.10

SCRUMstudy ScrumMaster Certified (SMC) Eligibility Requirements

Requirements	Description
Education	None
Experience	Prefer a SDC certified professional
Eligibility criteria	Anyone who is interested in becoming a ScrumMaster

SCRUMSTUDY SCRUMMASTER CERTIFIED (SMC)*

The ScrumMaster Certified professionals are organizers who ensure that a Scrum team is given an environment that is favorable to successful project completion. This is a servant leader role where the ScrumMaster provides guidance; facilitates and teaches Scrum practices to a project team. This role removes obstacles and ensures that team members adhere to Scrum practices as required. Table 13.10 provides the list of eligibility requirements for the SMC.

SCRUMSTUDY AGILE EXPERT CERTIFIED (AEC)†

The Agile Expert Certified credential holder has the capability to compare and choose the appropriate agile method in any given circumstance. As a result of fast changes in information technology, market demands, and expectations, the road has been paved to support the implementation of agile methods in many organizations. Agility depends upon adaptive planning and iterative development and delivery. The focus of agile is the amount of value provided by a project team in getting the work done efficiently. Table 13.11 provides a list of eligibility requirements for this credential.

TABLE 13.11

SCRUMstudy Agile Expert Certified (AEC) Eligibility Requirements

Requirements	Description
Education	Prefer an SDC™ (or) SMC™ certified professional
Experience	None
Eligibility criteria	Anyone on a Scrum team

* SCRUMstudy. (2014b).
† SCRUMstudy. (2014c).

TABLE 13.12

SCRUMstudy Scrum Product Owner Certified (SPOC) Eligibility Requirements

Requirements	Description
Education	Prefer a SDC™ (or) SMC™ certified professional
Experience	None
Eligibility criteria	Anyone who interfaces with project stakeholders or works as a Product Owner in a Scrum project

SCRUMSTUDY SCRUM PRODUCT OWNER CERTIFIED (SPOC)[*]

The Product Owner's role is to represent the interests of all stakeholders on the Scrum team. This role ensures accurate communication concerning the product or service functionality or features, user stories, or acceptance criteria and verifying that the criteria have been satisfied. The SPOC must be understanding and supportive of the needs and interests of every stakeholder as well as the Scrum team. Table 13.12 outlines the eligibility requirements for this role.

SCRUMSTUDY EXPERT SCRUMMASTER (ESM)[†]

The Expert ScrumMaster is an advanced certification for Scrum practitioners who wish to achieve an advanced level of expertise in Scrum. The attainment of this credential shows that the holder has the capability to manage complex Scrum projects and is able to scale Scrum in multifaceted situations with large project teams, programs, and portfolios. Table 13.13 lists the eligibility requirements for the credential.

TABLE 13.13

SCRUMstudy Expert ScrumMaster (ESM) Eligibility Requirements

Requirements	Description
Education	Expected to be a SMC™, AEC™, and SPOC™ certified
Experience	Three years managing Scrum/agile projects
Eligibility criteria	Experienced Scrum professional

---

[*] SCRUMstudy. (2014d).
[†] SCRUMstudy. (2014e).

TABLE 13.14

SCRUMstudy Certified Trainer (SCT) Eligibility Requirements

Requirements	Description
Education	Successfully pass three SCRUMstudy certifications exams (SDC, SMC, AEC, SPOC, and ESM)
	Must pass the certification course that the applicant wishes to teach
Experience	Two years of relevant work experience
	Willingness to share experiences in the courses that they teach
Eligibility criteria	All trainers should be associated with a SCRUMstudy Registered Education Provider (REP)
	Must be aware of training resources in the SCRUMstudy REP

SCRUMSTUDY CERTIFIED TRAINER (SCT)*

This credential requires that training for SCRUMstudy certification exams be conducted in classrooms or with virtual instructor-led sessions. Every trainer is expected to be at the expert level in the certification that he wishes to teach. The other option is to be extremely knowledgeable with the material in the *Scrum Body of Knowledge (SBOK^{TM}) Guide*. The trainer must have good people skills and consistently deliver high-quality training sessions. Table 13.14 lists the eligibility requirements for this credential.

CHAPTER SUMMARY

This concludes our discussion of agile certifications. This list may or may not be all inclusive, however, the author believes that sufficient information has been provided for those who are considering certifications in agile methods.

---

* SCRUMstudy. (2014f).

14

Agile Contracts

The agile contract is different from traditional contracts in that scope, costs, and the amount of value to be delivered are somewhat tricky to calculate up front. It is highly probable that a detailed description is not present in the agile contract because of frequent changes on these types of projects. We need to address the agile value, *"Customer collaboration over contract negotiation,"* in order to truly understand the intent of agile contracting.

The main idea is to build the contract around the end product rather than adding in a placeholder for unknown changes. Readers are reminded that agile methods are conducive to a great deal of flexibility which allows for the accommodation of changing requirements and priority levels. As a result, creating acceptance criteria on agile contracts can be a cause of concern on the vendor side. We need to understand that agile projects support static costs and time; however, product scope is always going to be very dynamic. Why? The project must deliver high-priority, top-quality product features first under resource and time restrictions. This all boils down to the fact that the customer could possibly have (bad idea on the agile project) fixed prices and scope, but the estimates will be padded with an uncertainty buffer included in the price. From the customer perspective, the downside to this contracting rationale is they may end up paying for non-valued-added activities after the project is completed.

There also needs to be a certain amount of trust between the parties involved in the contract, otherwise it will be difficult for some vendors to accept. Creating a trusting relationship on agile projects requires vendors to be on-site, hands-on, and involved. If there is trust, then the expectation is that the end client will gain a competitive edge as a result of high value added at reasonable (preferably low) costs. The vendor, however, expects high profits and low risks which would mean that both parties have to meet at a middle ground. Agile contracting is not a sound idea for the client–vendor relationship where there are no face-to-face interactions or trust. We will now discuss several contract types that are designed just for agile projects.

STORY POINT BILLING MODEL*

A story point is a comparative measure of project work. For example, an agile team may decide that it takes one story point to complete a task. The team has previously agreed that one story point equates to one hour of work. From that basis, two story points equate to two hours of work. Readers need to understand that the agile team decides the value of a story point. Another example would be that the agile team agrees that one story point is equal to one day of work. The value of a story point is decided and agreed upon by the agile team, but the developers have the most input into what a story point actually amounts to because they are the ones building the product. A story point could equate to a day, a week, or even a month based on what the team decides to use as the basis.

The story point billing model was designed as a win–win contracting solution for both the vendor and the customer. This model is based on using story points as the basis for calculating costs on the agile projects. The customer is charged only for the actual number of story points that are delivered as "done" within iterations. To clarify how story points can be used to bill the customer, let's say, for example, that a story point represents one hour of work. One hour of work costs $50.00. If the team has developed 100 story points at $50.00 and the customer agrees on the price, then the customer is billed for (100 times $50.00) which equals to $5,000.00. Let us begin by explaining how this model is calculated. There are three steps involved:

1. *Formulate the triangulation wall used for estimation.* There are three sides to the triangulation wall. Triangulation is used to estimate a user story based on a story's relationship to other stories. Triangulate means "to divide into triangles." Because triangles are three sided, we use three areas against which to form our estimates:

---

* Scrum Alliance. (2013).

    a. With traditional project management model the three sides are:
       1. Scope (fixed)
       2. Time (varied)
       3. Costs (varied)
    b. With the agile model, the three sides are:
       1. Costs (fixed)
       2. Time (fixed)
       3. Scope (varied)

A wall is considered to be a set of standard tasks for a story within a particular type of technology and purview. For example, we are building a product web application that receives data from two distinct sources. A story in this example would have requirements to import data from the two sources and then create a report. The resultant user story might be worth two story points (because of two data sources) for an example. This is how the user story could be mapped to the triangulation wall item(s) in regard to how many resources, how much time, and what functionality.

2. *Calculate story point and dollar conversions.* Once the triangulation wall is established, the cost of developing a story point must be calculated. This would be a time-boxed phase based on agreement by all parties. The actual costs of developing a story point can be calculated based on the number of stories accepted and the amount of money expended during iterations. The billing model is at this point a story point model.

3. *Define the scope of the iteration(s).* The scope determines how much revenue the vendor can generate based on the story points. The vendor may only bill the customer based on the number of accepted story points per iteration. This provides for a consistent generation of income for the vendor. The scope determines the number of story points within the iteration. Let's say, for example, that the scope of a single iteration is 55 story points. The vendor and customer agree that a single story point costs $100 to develop. The scope calculated in dollars for this particular iteration would be $5,500.

The story point billing model is indeed a win–win situation for both the customer and vendor. The customer is satisfied with high value being delivered quickly and frequently, and the vendor generates revenue each time value is delivered under a unique billing model with relatively low risks. Readers are cautioned that this billing model may not be suited to all agile projects. The triangulation wall can be intimidating and complicated for some projects because of the requirements to convert story points into dollar equivalency. This model is recommended for the following types of agile projects:

- A project where the requirements are constantly changing
- A new product is being developed
- Spanking brand new agile vendor–customer relationship

MONEY FOR NOTHING AND CHANGE FOR FREE

According to Jeff Sutherland (2013) the "money for nothing and change for free" strategy has been widely adopted as the foundation for many agile contracts.* This contracting strategy is best for cases where a customer asks for an up-front estimate on an entire contract. Basically, this type of contract provides for early termination under certain conditions and is flexible when changes are needed on the project. Sounds good so far, right? In addition, this contract begins as a fixed price and it includes time and materials for any add-on work. A "change for free" option is included and this is where the contract terms get interesting. This "change for free" clause can only be implemented by the customer in the case where the work is continued with the same team in place for all iterations and the customer is fully engaged. In the event this clause is voided, then the contract goes back to time and materials billing. If the customer stays with the same team and if the Product Owner wants to make changes at the end of an iteration (i.e., re-prioritize the product backlog), then these changes are free if and only if the total contract work has not changed (i.e., the scope has not changed). This results in additional items being added at zero costs.† In regards to the "money for nothing" clause, a customer has the right to terminate the contract at the end of any iteration. In the event that the customer feels that there is very little value in continuing the project, he or she has the right to terminate the contract and pay the vendor 20% of the remaining contract as the penalty for ending the project. This

---

* Sutherland, J. (2013).
† Griffiths, M. (2012).

is considered to be "money for nothing" because the vendor is getting paid and the work will have ended. Readers must understand that at this point, the customer would have already used up 80% of the project budget. At any time when the customer fails to fully participate in the iterations and/ or the parties are unable to agree on costing, the contract rates return to time and material billing. Let's elaborate a little more for a detailed understanding of what this agile contract type entails.

The "change for free" clause in the contract can only be executed if the customer continues to work with the "same" team on every iteration for the project. This in essence means that the customer is doing what he or she should be doing as per this type of contract. In the case where the team changes, this contract clause is completely voided and the contract is now considered to have a time and material basis. On the other hand, if the customer continues to be engaged as required, the Product Owner can begin to reprioritize the backlog at the end of an iteration. The "change for free" clause is executed if the customer continues to participate in all of the iterations for the entire project. This affords the customer the right to make changes to the project's scope without any additional costs **if and only if** the total scope of work has not changed. New features can be legally added for free if items with equal scope are eliminated from the contract. The customer "has" to be engaged and has the right to cancel the project early in the case where it is believed that there is inadequate return on investment (ROI) in the product backlog for additional iterations. The vendor can decide to agree to the contract termination during any period of time for 20% of the outstanding contract value.

This 20% is the "money for nothing" feature of the contract and it is designed to mitigate the risk of dealing with an idle agile team. The customer gets 80% of high value, the project is completed earlier than planned, the vendor gets 20% of the remaining contract value as a bonus (including the 80%) for the completed work, and everyone is happy! The money for nothing contract clause gives the customer an opportunity to cancel the project early if it is believed that there is insufficient ROI in the backlog. This would mean that no additional iterations will take place. If needed at a later time, additional releases can be added through time and materials billing. This contract type allows for a great deal of flexibility in making changes on the agile project. It begins with a fixed price contract, includes a time and material clause for additional work, and it includes the "change for free" and "money for nothing" contract clauses.

FIXED PRICE CONTRACTS

There are other types of fixed price contracts that are used on agile projects such as:

- *Graduated Fixed Price Contract:* The hourly rate is based on finishing early (highest rate), finishing on time (second highest rate), or finishing late (lowest rate). For example, the rates are graduated as $150/hour, $130/hour, and $120/hour.
  - If the work is completed early, then the customer is happy because the overall price is lower as a result of fewer hours used.
  - However, if the project is late, then the vendor gets paid more overall, because of a higher number of hours used at a lower bill rate. Both parties are sharing the risks and the rewards based on the delivery schedule.
  - If the vendor delivers early, then the customer is satisfied because of fewer overall costs. The vendor in this case is happy as well because of a higher profit margin.
  - When the vendor delivers late, their bill rate is the lowest and they might possibly be displeased. The vendor will get paid more in overall costs because of having to use more hours, but with a lower profit margin. The customer in this case has to pay more in overall costs and may also be displeased.
- *Fixed Price Work Packages Contract:* This is a contract where the work is broken down into fixed price work packages. The first question would be, "Why do we need this?" This type of contract mitigates risks associated with under- or overestimating a piece of work by decreasing both scope and costs for the work that is being estimated. For example, a company can break down their statements of work (SOW) into distinct work packages where each has a fixed price. During the course of work, the vendor has the opportunity to estimate the work packages again as a result of the identification of new information and risks. The customer has the chance to revisit the prioritization of the work that is left based on developing costs. The vendor has the chance to update costs when new details present themselves and the need to add contingency costs is no longer relevant. Any additional changes that are pertinent can then be added

into the work packages. In the case where extra funds are actually needed, it won't be difficult or questionable to do so at any particular point of time going forward.

CHAPTER SUMMARY

It is not uncommon in the agile world for customers and vendors to create custom-built contracts that support a project's specific needs. In these cases, the customer retains the right to reprioritize the product backlog and eliminate the need for vendors to add contingency costs to the total contract price. Both the customer and the vendor are protected when using customized agile contract types.

15

Which Projects Should Be Agile?

Globally, many organizations have had struggles with troubled information technology software development projects. As a result, some of these organizations have made attempts to experiment with newer approaches such as agile methods with the expectation that value could be delivered early alongside superior quality features. The hope was that this change in approach would certainly result in more satisfied stakeholders. The author believes that agility has fulfilled its promise. Many projects have obtained successful outcomes with agile implementations. On the other hand, there are some organizations that are very cautious about forging ahead with agile. This guarded approach is based upon the acknowledgment that the agile framework is not appropriate for every project. This chapter identifies those types of projects that are suitable for agile and those that are not. We also provide simple techniques that can be used to make formal assessments when contemplating the move to agile methods.

AGILE VERSUS WATERFALL

How does an organization know when to select agile rather than the waterfall model for software development? The answer is not always simple. According to Ambadapudi Sridhara Murthy (2013), there are alternatives to waterfall and agile. Often a combination of both methods will yield the desired models as outlined below:

- *Agile in Waterfall:* The waterfall method does not typically allow for an immediate return on investment (ROI) and results are generally not seen until after the project has been completed. Once the product

TABLE 15.1

Agile in Waterfall

← Agile in Waterfall →				
Waterfall—All functionality is developed and released at one time.				
Requirements →	Design →	Execution →	Testing →	Release
← Agile in Waterfall—Overall waterfall and features developed and released with Agile →				
Requirements →	Feature 1 ↓	Feature 2 ↓	Feature 3 ↓	Feature 4 ↓
	Design	Design	Design	Design
	Execution	Execution	Execution	Execution
	Testing	Testing	Testing	Testing
	Release	Release	Release	Release

is finally made available, sometimes results are not as expected. The costs required to correct defects late in the life cycle are quite expensive when compared to fixing these issues earlier. Some organizations are not completely satisfied with the waterfall model because they want to see the result of the product more frequently, just like with the agile model. The solution would be to mix the waterfall method with agile and here's how this occurs. The project would begin with the waterfall method and then the requirements broken into components during the traditional schedule work breakdown process. Next, individual features would be broken down and developed with the agile method. Table 15.1 provides an example of how agile can be integrated with the waterfall methodology.

- *As-Needed Hybrid Model:* This model represents a combination of waterfall, agile, rapid application development (RAD), Extreme (XP), and so on. The idea behind the hybrid model is that an organization can continue to use their usual models and then gradually begin to adapt and move to the new model(s). A particular model is selected based upon its perceived execution speed, low risk ranking, and the expected quality level of the delivered product. It must be clear that

TABLE 15.2

Hybrid Model

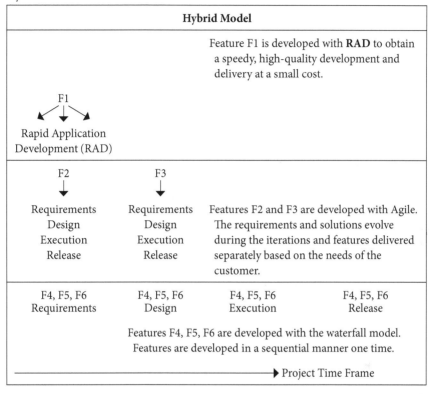

Hybrid Model			
		Feature F1 is developed with **RAD** to obtain a speedy, high-quality development and delivery at a small cost.	
F1 Rapid Application Development (RAD)			
F2 ↓	F3 ↓		
Requirements Design Execution Release	Requirements Design Execution Release	Features F2 and F3 are developed with Agile. The requirements and solutions evolve during the iterations and features delivered separately based on the needs of the customer.	
F4, F5, F6 Requirements	F4, F5, F6 Design	F4, F5, F6 Execution	F4, F5, F6 Release
Features F4, F5, F6 are developed with the waterfall model. Features are developed in a sequential manner one time.			
→ Project Time Frame			

although an organization makes plans to use the hybrid model, it is recommended to continue to use the methods they have become accustomed to and then slowly add agile into the mix along with other methods as appropriate. Table 15.2 depicts the structure of the hybrid model.

• *Waterfall within Agile:* There are some organizations that criticize agile methods for lack of documentation and the quality of the product. Say what? Some folks feel that agile projects are quality and documentation deficient and that this would leave the organization in a place where they would be unable to take the proper corrective actions at later times. The remedy for this perceived dilemma can be rectified by the usage of the waterfall model during the iterations. See Table 15.3 for a description of this adapted model.

As most of us are aware, organizations are under tremendous pressure to deliver projects faster within budget and scope. In addition, the

TABLE 15.3

Waterfall in Agile

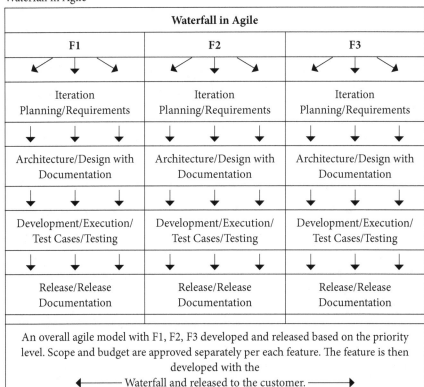

Waterfall in Agile		
F1	**F2**	**F3**
Iteration Planning/Requirements	Iteration Planning/Requirements	Iteration Planning/Requirements
Architecture/Design with Documentation	Architecture/Design with Documentation	Architecture/Design with Documentation
Development/Execution/ Test Cases/Testing	Development/Execution/ Test Cases/Testing	Development/Execution/ Test Cases/Testing
Release/Release Documentation	Release/Release Documentation	Release/Release Documentation

An overall agile model with F1, F2, F3 developed and released based on the priority level. Scope and budget are approved separately per each feature. The feature is then developed with the ◄——— Waterfall and released to the customer. ———►

expectation is to provide all of the functionality that a customer desires within the smallest number of releases possible. As a result of projects with compressed time frames, companies feel that they are required to forge ahead with agile methods without doing proper evaluations to determine whether this process is a best fit. It must be clear that agile is not a fit for every project and it is the responsibility of an organization to conduct the proper analysis prior to the selection of this method.

AGILE NOT A FIT

According to Barrington Rowe (2014), agile is not a proper solution for the following types of projects:

- A project that requires changes to complex code that has been written with unstructured programming practices is not a good agile candidate. This would be the case of older legacy systems with tightly coupled code such as functions or classes that are very dependent upon each other and require a lot of effort to modify. In contrast, code that is loosely coupled is not dependent upon other code.
- A potential project where the release management process is very costly. In addition, the time and effort required for a production deployment is extreme. As a result of cost concerns an organization is led to believe that a single release is the best option. However, limiting a product to a single release because of cost concerns is not practical.
- A project where the team lacks experience and skills required for complex user stories. This would mean that some user stories would need to be implemented over multiple iterations. The recommendation is that a user story be completed within a single iteration. In addition, a skills gap is a real risk to any project.
- A project where the risk of having a third-party vendor as a major stakeholder is high. This is the case of the vendor having responsibility for providing products or services that are critical. If a vendor does not deliver as required, a dreadful scheduling mishap would have the potential to affect the project negatively. Another risk is user stories that depend upon this type of vendor and they are delayed until later iterations: a definite no-no.
- A project that has user stories that are inadequate for whatever reason (untestable, no value, not estimatable, independent, or non-negotiable). This would be a huge risk to the project.

Furthermore, an organization is advised to use decision-making tools and techniques as discussed in this chapter to determine which projects are proper candidates for agile implementation. Just as a project is evaluated for its potential to be chosen carefully over others, this same concept should be applied to determine if a project is an "agile candidate." During the analysis process of determining which projects are good candidates for agility, a determination should be made as to what changes need to take place so that impediments can be removed. Once changes are made, the project can move forward to being categorized as "agile appropriate."

With regard to changes that may need to be made, organizations need to consider whether their existing IT unit is grounded on the waterfall lifecycle model. An organization should never attempt to place traditional IT personnel in the agile environment without proper training and expect an automatic success story. It would be a drastic change for these workers to become cross-functional without guidance and understanding of the agile requirements. It is well known that organizational changes are often prolonged and painful for many companies. Change is not easy for everyone to accept. We must understand that agile implementation requires a cultural change within an organization that should not be undertaken lightly.

AGILE FIT OR MISFIT?

Many organizations are not able to comprehend fully some of the challenges that occur during their transition to the agile framework. Most are attempting to make a direct change from the waterfall to agile methods. There are other situations where agile is a good fit and other circumstances where the method is considered to be a misfit. We now describe the best project type for agile methods.

Murthy (2013) provides a very specific circumstance for agile success: web-enabled technologies. He goes on to restate that agile methods support changing requirements throughout a project. The fact that defects are revealed during continuous iterations means that there is never a wait to review these types of discrepancies. Changes and fixes are included in the code during the next iteration after being discovered. This ultimately results in a reduction in costs that are associated with resolving defects. In addition, there is no impact on the product's delivery date with this approach.

Murthy (2013) further states that agile is a dynamic model and when used properly typically results in a success story. In spite of the fact that most agile projects are undoubtedly successful, there are occasions where agile projects sometimes fail. The question is why? The answer is quite simple: if an agile project is not implemented properly, the end result is a "sunken" project that undoubtedly would need to be redone. Ouch! Murthy (2013) goes on to describe several reasons why agile projects fail:

- *People—attitude and beliefs:* In very simple terms, team members with the "me" attitude are a contributing factor to failure on the agile project. The attitude should always be "we" because the entire team is equally responsible for the success or failure of the agile project.

Being motivated as a single entity is a driving force behind successful product delivery and the attainment of the project's goals.

- *Team expertise, servant leader:* It is critical that the agile team is established with the right level of expertise. Inexperienced developers are not appropriate for this type of team. This team needs enthusiasm, exceptional skills, and self-motivation. Concerning the servant leader (a ScrumMaster, e.g.), this role needs to understand how to serve the agile team as well as provide leadership.
- *Product owner—understanding of role and responsibilities:* A major success factor for the agile project is the Product Owner's role and the level of understanding required in terms of engaging with stakeholders and managing the product backlog. If this role is not able to provide clarification for the user stories so that the development team can build the product, the agile team will undoubtedly experience failure and frustration.
- *Documentation:* Murthy (2013) asserts that there are critical documentation areas with the potential to harm an agile project in the long term. In cases where a developer(s) might leave the project, then all of the information could be lost if there is no documentation to pass on to new team members. We know that there is some documentation that is required on the agile project such as user stories and design artifacts. What if team members on the agile project have the false belief that no documentation is ever required? The author believes that this misconception would be disastrous.
- *Schedule, budgets, and contracts:* According to Griffiths (2012), agile projects typically work under fixed time and costs. Scope has to be dynamic and can never be static in this case. We must understand that whenever scope is static, there is a risk that time or money can be exhausted prior to the product being delivered. This can also increase the probability that the product will be of insufficient quality. As a result of frequent and unplanned changes, an increase in scope would cause an upsurge in the budget and time frame for the agile project. This would mean that a traditional fixed price contract should never be used. This is a major factor of agile project failure because some organizations are not clear on the implementation and have frequently utilized the incorrect contract type. A fixed price contract is not flexible enough for agile methods because the team would be limited by the budget. This constraint has the potential for the team to lose sight of delivering a quality product.

LIMITATIONS OF AGILE SOFTWARE PROCESSES*

According to Turk, France, and Rumpe (2002), there are definite limitations associated with some of the agile software processes. Notice that we have referred only to the processes and not the actual agile methods. This distinction is clearly important and Turk et al. (2002) acknowledge that agile methods differ in their values, practices, and application domains. As a result, it is not an easy task to evaluate all of the agile processes in a general sense and apply these limitations across the board. This study and analysis originated using several XP projects as a source. The assumptions were made from the following agile methods:

- Extreme Programming (XP)
- Scrum
- Agile Unified Process
- Agile Modeling
- Agile Alliance Principles

Following is a list of the limitations that were uncovered by Turk et al. (2002) for agile software processes:

- *Limited provision for dispersed development environment:* Agile methods support colocated environments. This can be alleged as a hindrance to those organizations desiring to develop software in globally dispersed environments. An alternative solution is video conferencing, however, this can be very expensive depending upon the number of people involved.
- *Restricted support for subcontracting:* The subcontracting process requires that requirements in the contract be clearly defined in adequate detail so that costs can be accurately estimated. Agile methods are adaptive and are not predictive enough for some subcontracting purposes. In Chapter 14 we have spoken of the need to have agile contracts on agile projects. Turk et al. (2002) recommend a two-part contract: fixed and variable.
  - Fixed Part: This is the portion that outlines the framework limiting how the subcontractor includes changes into the product.

---

* Turk, D., France, R., and Rumpe, B. (2002).

It also includes what the subcontractor must do, and what must be delivered.

- Variable Part: This is the portion that outlines the requirements and deliverables that will change within the boundaries of the fixed part of the contract. Variation is expected but within the boundaries of what has been established as fixed. Prioritized items should be included in this section during the time the contract is executed.

- *Limited support for the construction of recyclable items:* Agile methods are concentrated on building products for specific solutions that are not generic enough to be used on other projects. In the past, it was very desirable for software components to be developed that could be used in other software products. There is no clear understanding as to how agile processes could be adapted for recyclable software components when the goal is to develop a certain product for a specific customer.

- *Limited development support when using large teams:* The agile process supports small- to medium-sized teams rather than large teams. Communication becomes less effective with a large-sized team as a result of face-to-face practices. Large teams need less informal agile and more formal processes to tackle bigger projects. The level of agility has the potential to be smaller in large-team environments and bigger in smaller team environments.

- *Limited support for building safety-critical software:* According to Turk et al. (2002), in the case of safety-critical software where failure would cause the loss of human life or catastrophic economic repercussions, the agile process does not have adequate quality control processes in place that could provide assurances of protection from disaster. Critical components of software should be developed under more formal software development methods.

- *Limited support for building large software systems:* Code refactoring can be very expensive for large systems. Some systems have components that are not very easy to modify because they are critical to the essential services that are offered. Some systems have functionality that is so tightly coupled and intertwined that it may be impossible to develop software incrementally. Code that is developed using an iterative methodology may be fit for use, however, when used in each iteration, all of the components will be in dissimilar and incomplete stages.

AGILE CHALLENGES[*]

We now focus our attention on agile challenges: perceived, imagined, or real. Gandomani et al. (2013) have identified several aspects of agile methods that could be viewed as challenges which need to be overcome prior to moving to agile methods. The author would like readers to be cognizant of the fact that a subjective analysis has been provided for the ratings of each challenge (perceived, imagined, or real). Other experts may have different views on these areas of concern.

1. *People.*
   a. Senior-level developers have a particular mind-set that is often perceived as being difficult or at times impossible to change (perceived and real).
   b. Difficulties with implementing pair programming in XP with senior-level developers (real).
   c. Code ownership is a challenge from the developer's viewpoint when compared to other types of teams (perceived).
   d. Overly ambitious people have been known to alter a customer's priorities that make the transition to agile more difficult (perceived and real).
   e. Cultural differences can be barriers when transitioning to agile methods (real).
   f. Communication complications within some organizations could affect the move to agile methods (real).
2. *Management.*
   a. A self-organizing team is sometimes difficult to establish for some organizations (both real and perceived).
   b. Lack of solid agile change management strategy (perceived).
   c. Agile team roles may be very difficult for some companies to fill (real and/or imagined).
   d. Some project managers who have backgrounds in traditional software development are not able to let go of former roles and responsibilities easily and may find the transition to the servant leader role "uncomfortable" (real).

---

[*] Gandomani, T. J., Zulzalil, H., Ghani, A. A. A., and Sultan, A. B. M. (2013).

e. There are some who believe that a perfect customer is a fairy tale. The customer is required to take on a servant leader role and must drive the agile process by taking responsibility for the prioritized product backlog. Some feel that this is a stretch to get a customer to move into this role easily (perceived).

f. Lack of qualified agile coaches can be a challenge (real).

g. From a management point of view, little or no documentation can be a hindrance to project success (perceived).

h. Team decision making may be flawed as a result of:

  i. Lack of readiness to commit to decisions because of prior reliance on the project manager (real).

  ii. Conflicting priorities (real).

  iii. Unstable resource obtainability (real).

  iv. Lack of implementation decisions by team members (real).

  v. Unwillingness to take ownership (real).

  vi. Lack of team empowerment by blocking experts from making decisions (perceived).

  vii. Team decision making with regard to resource provision, strategic product line positioning, development, and maintenance work requirements can be obstacles during the adoption of agile methods (real).

3. *Process.*

  a. Moving from a traditional model to an iterative model can be challenging for some organizations. This transition can be a genuine obstacle because this is a big change that has a huge impact on business strategies, tools, methods, and roles (real).

  b. Colocated teams can be an obstacle for distributed organizations (real).

  c. Different ways of measurement in agile and traditional practices can be perceived as issues for anyone prejudiced against traditional processes (perceived).

4. *Technology.*

  a. Differences in the degrees of agility are perceived to be unequal across the agile methods (real).

  b. Agile methods focus on either software development or project management (real).

  c. Lack of knowledge regarding the capabilities of specific agile methods (real).

TABLE 15.4

Agile Suitability Construct

Agile Suitability Construct				
Practices	Have ⟶	Limitations		Suitability of Agile methods
Organizational culture and personnel capabilities	determine ⟶	Organizational capability to handle agility effectively	⟶	

IS AGILE SUITABLE?

Van Dijk (2011) acknowledges that there is only a small amount of theoretical information available to assist practitioners during their analysis and selection process for an appropriate agile methodology. An assertion was made that an appropriate framework is not one that should be modified to fit all circumstances. The right framework should be flexible in such a way that it is inclusive of various points of view that have been established upon the existing methods as required. In order to actually determine if a particular method is right, the framework would need to include:

- The project characteristics
- Agile characteristics
- The relationship between the project and agile characteristics
- A technique that can be used to evaluate these characteristics (the project and agile) so that a decision can be made

In order to accomplish the objectives listed above, the following suitability construct has been established and recommended by Van Dijk (2011) as identified in Table 15.4.

Agile Suitability Construct

Let's begin our discussion of the suitability construct so that the proper understanding is obtained as to how we utilize it for actual projects. According to Van Dijk (2011), whenever we examine the available agile methods that are currently available, we must consider the following contingency factors:

- The capabilities of agile methods are expressed in terms of limitations.
- The capabilities of organizations are expressed in terms of culture and personnel capabilities (Table 15.4).

The suitability construct can be used to make a decision by conducting an evaluation of the environment for the project by providing answers to the following questions (Van Dijk, 2011):

1. *What are the limitations that apply to the situation?* Van Dijk refers to the same limitations that have been identified by Turk et al. (2002) in the section "Limitations of Agile Software Processes" in this chapter.
2. *Is the organizational culture a hierarchical one?* Van Dijk asserts that a hierarchical organizational culture does not favor agile methods. Descriptions of his four cultural types are given below:
   - Group culture: Transformation and internal focus.
   - Development culture: Transformation and external factors.
   - Rational culture: Constancy and external focus.
   - Hierarchical culture: Constancy and internal focus.
3. *Does the organization presently use or has it had any past experience with agile components?*
   - An information system development (ISD) method component is agile if it contributes to one or more of the following:
     - Creates change.
     - Acts in anticipation of change.
     - Reacts to change.
     - Learns from change.
   - To be considered agile, an ISD method component must make a contribution to one or more of the following and must not take away from:
     - Alleged economy.
     - Alleged simplicity.
     - Alleged quality.
   - To be considered agile, an ISD method component must be continuously ready to prepare the component for usage (i.e., being ready refers to minimum time and costs).
4. *Is the capability of the organization's personnel suitable (Van Dijk, 2011)?* Following are descriptions and categories that identify the skill levels of an organization's personnel.
   - *Level 3:* Capability to modify a method (modifies the guidelines in order to apply the method to a new situation).

- *Level 2:* Capability to modify a method to fit a new situation.
- *Level 1A:* Capability to conduct optional method steps with training (estimate user stories to fit iterations, refactoring, etc.); with some experience, has the potential to be Level 2.
- *Level 1B:* Capability to conduct routine method steps with training (coding, simple refactoring, test execution, configuration management, etc.); with experience can perform some Level 1A skills.
- *Level 1:* Potential technical skills but unwilling to collaborate or adhere to shared methods.

Furthermore, Van Dijk (2011) states that a particular agile method is only superior to another when there are requirements to be agile and an organization has the capability to be agile. As we have previously stated in this chapter and Van Dijk concurs: organizations need to conduct proper assessments of their capabilities and prerequisites prior to the selection of an agile method.

AGILE IMPLEMENTATION: RISKS AND ISSUES

According to Veneziano, Rainer, and Haider (2014), there are several risks (or issues) that should be addressed prior to making a decision to "go agile" for a particular project. After examination of the items, the question would then be: "How could this potential risk factor affect our project?" Although the list does not include all possible factors, the items in Table 15.5 should be seriously considered. As previously stated in this chapter, an organization does have the option to make changes and remove impediments so that a project can be moved forward to the agile list. The reader should observe that the limitations asserted by Turk et al. (2002) are once again in force as shown in Table 15.5.

Agile Adoption Decision Model

Veneziano et al. (2014) implement an agile decision-making model (WAINGE) that uses each issue/risk factor (r), that has been weighted against a suggested value $(w)^*$ that makes a contribution to the calculation

---

[*] The project team needs to agree upon the range to be used based on decimals between the range of 0 and 1.

TABLE 15.5

WAINGE Agile Decision Maker v1.8

		WAINGE AGILE DECISION MAKER v. 1.8	
Item #	Risk Factor (*r*)	Description	Weights (*w*)
1	1	Customer cannot be available for the entire duration of the development process.	0.8
2	1	An incomplete user acceptance test is highly probable.	0.8
3	1	An unreliable estimate on time and budget is expected.	0.7
4	1	Documentation is not thoroughly developed and not a critical asset.	0.8
5	1	Some agile methodologies and practices have the potential to be less flexible than anticipated by an overall agile approach.	0.6
6	1	Lack of experience and the relaxed discipline of agile have the potential to affect project management negatively.	0.5
7	1	Lack of support for distributed development environments has the potential to occur.	0.0
8	1	Outsourcing or subcontracting will probably be more problematic to accomplish.	0.0
9	1	Support and opportunities for developing reusable objects is limited.	1.0
10	1	Limited or unsustainable support for development with large teams.	0.0
11	1	Limited support for developing safety-critical software is expected to occur.	0.5
12	1	Limited support for developing large multifarious software is expected to occur.	0.8
13	1	Insufficient focus on architecture has the potential to produce less than desired design decisions.	1.0
14	1	As a result of the social values that agile embraces, there is a potential for decision making to be less than desired.	0.6

continued

TABLE 15.5 (continued)

WAINGE Agile Decision Maker v1.8

Item #	Risk Factor (r)	Description	Weights (w)
15	1	High turnover is expected for agile developers and consultants.	0.9
16	1	There is a perception that agile methods only wrestle with trivial components of a project and leave the complex ones unaddressed.	0.8
17	1	The agile development process and results have the potential to rely on the quality of the people that have been hired.	0.7
18	1	There is a risk that adaptive planning could be interpreted as lack of long-term planning.	0.3
19	1	Planning poker, (a variation of wideband Delphi) and other decision-making approaches have the potential to be affected by unwilling team members who could be unfocused on actual development.	0.8

AVA	0.4		Explanation of Calculations		DEC	0.576583616
Note: AVA value is an input value and is not calculated.	**No. of Issues**	19	Input Value only (no calculations)		The final answer is .57 which rounds to 60%. Recall that any number greater than 50% is considered to be a high-risk agile project.	
	$(\Sigma r)/n$	0.610526316	= SUM (all weights (w)) divided by the total number of weights (19))			
	$\Delta = (1 - \Sigma r/n)$	0.389473684	= 1 – 0.610526316			
	MAF	–0.0339427	= LOG((0.5 + AVA)/ (1.5 – AVA)) * MIN(ABS(0.610526316), ABS(0.389473684))		**DEC = MAF + 0.610526316**	

Source: Derived from V. Veneziano, A. W. Rainer, and S. Haider, *When Agile Is Not Good Enough: An Initial Attempt at Understanding How to Make the Right Decision.* University of Hertfordshire: School of Computer Science, pp. 1–10, 2014. With permission.

of the overall risk ranking for the implementation of an agile method. The overall specific risk (OSR) is a value between 0 and 1 and it can be defined as the sum of the (*n*) risk factors associated with each issue from the critical items list (again please refer to Table 15.5). The result should be a number that can be used to make a decision on the overall risk ranking for adopting agile for a particular project. The author of this book was able to obtain the actual WAINGE model and found it very useful and easy to comprehend. We now provide more detail regarding the agile usability model.

WAINGE Model

This model has been developed in MS Excel and, according to Veneziano et al. (2014), can be requested directly from the creator. The name WAINGE is derived from the title of their paper, "When Agile Is Not Good Enough: An Initial Attempt at Understanding How to Make the Right Decision." The model's usage starts with the input of the AVA value.

Attitude Value toward Agile (AVA)

The attitude value toward agile (AVA) is to be measured against an entire development team; the values obtained are between 0 and 1 where:

- 0 = An extreme agile critic
- 0.5 = An ideal neutral view
- 1 = An extreme agile supporter

Risk Factors for Agile Adoption

For usability purposes, and during the research, the risk factor (*r*) value for the adoption of agile on projects was always assumed to be 1 (Veneziano et al., 2014). In addition, weights (*w*) were assigned for all 19 risk factors and are based upon the following:

- 1 = Very high impact
- 0 = Very low impact

Mitigation Amplification Factor (MAF)

We now describe the mitigation amplification factor (MAF) as the value that represents the team's attitude (as a myth) and is used to standardize the decisional value that has been derived from the overall specific risk. The question used to obtain the MAF is, "*Do you describe yourself and your team as agile supporters?*" The resultant answer should be between:

- 0 = Absolutely no
- 1 = Absolutely yes

The response provided from the MAF above is used to calibrate the decisional tool against the attitudes of stakeholders. It must be understood that the researchers somewhat transformed the curve (i.e., inverse hyperbolic tangent) in order to better accommodate the values of the MAF to fall within the expected ranges of 0 to 1 for the final DEC value (Veneziano et al., 2014).

Final Decisional Value

The final decisional value (DEC) will always be a value between 0 and 1, which can be converted into a percentage. A DEC > 0.5 represents the threshold that would indicate that the adoption of any agile method is very risky; however, this premise should be further authenticated by observable evidence. In addition, the DEC is calculated by the sum of the overall risk plus the mitigation factor depending upon whether the team's attitude is for or against agile (Veneziano et al., 2014). Once again, the reader is encouraged to study Table 15.5 in order to gain an understanding of how the WAINGE model is used to provide an agile ready decision. Better yet and as previously mentioned, the MS Excel spreadsheet that contains the WAINGE model can be requested from its creators. Readers are encouraged to make this request for complete analysis. The model's implementation is very straightforward.

CHAPTER SUMMARY

We have identified two methods of determining whether a project is an agile candidate. Our intent was to provide relatively simple tools and techniques that can be used on actual projects. Even though tools are helpful, it is up to the organization to decide how and when to move forward with the agile methods. We hope that readers have found the information useful.

16

Agile Change Management

As we have previously mentioned throughout this book, agile methods are cognizant of the fact that requirements change quite often. The agile framework embraces changes to user stories, design, and other deliverables at any time during the project. Modifications represent a way to provide value and are accepted in order to enhance the customer's competitive advantage. Change is never frowned upon and the agile team never fails to embrace modifications. We need to be mindful of the fact that changes can be rejected on rare occasions, but only in circumstances where a proposed change does not add any value for the customer. Flexibility is the nature of the agile beast, no pun intended. In this chapter, we describe how agile practitioners manage and accept change throughout the iterations.

AGILE CHANGE MANAGEMENT PROCESS

The approach to agile change management should be flexible and simplified. We have previously discussed the fact that the agile project is required to build products that have a great amount of value and quality. The way to accomplish this feat is to build the highest priority features prior to addressing those that have a low priority. We must remember that this prioritization system realizes an early return on investment (ROI) and a satisfied stakeholder experience. Let us now list the process steps that address changes to the requirements. The author expects that the process that follows will be quite familiar to the reader. See Table 16.1 for details.

Readers should recognize that the six steps in Table 16.1 represent the normal processes of managing changes to requirements under the umbrella for agile methods. This is an inherent process that manages

TABLE 16.1

Agile Change Management Process

Step #	Description	Changes
1.	The user stories that have the highest priority or risk levels are selected by the Product Owner and/or stakeholders for the "first" or the next iteration.	No changes made to requirements yet.
2.	As the work items (user stories) are added to the product backlog, they are prioritized by the Product Owner and/or stakeholders.	Changes are made at this point by adding a priority level.
3.	These prioritized user stories are given greater detail so that they can be built.	Changes are made to requirements at this point by adding more detail.
4.	The development team then selects user stories from the high-priority list only for the next iteration. The development team creates tasks for the user stories.	Changes are made to requirements at this point by creating estimates to complete the work and/or adding story points.
5.	As necessary, the work items are reprioritized where the assigned priority levels are made higher or lower.	This is where changes are made in the requirements as they are reprioritized and previous priority levels are altered.
6.	This process repeats until all iterations and releases are complete.	n/a

changes to the requirements during maintenance of the product backlog. In addition, please refer to Figure 16.1 for a visual representation of how changes are managed on the agile project.

Reasons That Requirements Change

According to Ambler (2014), there are many reasons for requirement changes on the agile project. Table 16.2 lists common reasons for these actions.

Importance of Agile Change Management[*]

Why is change management important? The better question for this book is: "Why is agile change management important?" As the reader may recall, agile is all about providing value to the customer. Agile change management is also focused on value. Value is an agile driver. Organizations must

---

[*] Dalipi, F., Rufati, E., and Idrizi, F. (2013).

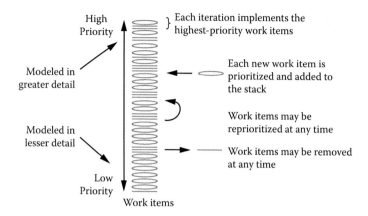

FIGURE 16.1

Agile change management process.

TABLE 16.2

Reasons for Requirement Changes

Reason	Description
1. Requirement was inadvertently left out.	There will be times where a stakeholder may come to the realization that a particular feature or functionality was missed during the elicitation process.
2. Defect identification.	A need to correct a defect can warrant the addition of a new or modified requirement.
3. Not as desired requirement.	A stakeholder may come to the realization that what they asked for in terms of a requirement was not what was desired. This would result in a new or modified requirement.
4. Political motivation.	As a result of changing priorities, requirements can warrant changes.
5. Market conditions.	Competition may warrant functionality that is needed to level the playing field in the marketplace.
6. Legal requirements.	A new law or changes to an existing law can require changes in software functionality.

Source: Derived from S. W. Ambler, *Agile Modeling: Agile Requirements Change Management.* Retrieved from http://www.agilemodeling.com/essays/changeManagement.htm 2014. With permission.

remain competitive in order to remain profitable and stay in business. Regarding change, this means that companies must manage and control change, otherwise change has the potential to result in uncertainty which in turn can result in greater risk. Many of us know where this story is going. It is very important that businesses understand how change affects

184 • Agile for Project Managers

their bottom line: profitability. Market conditions change frequently and this is a fact of life to which many business owners are quite accustomed. Ups and downs in the marketplace result in strategy changes, diverse marketing goals, product changes, and the list of impacts can get bigger and bigger.

Companies that adopt agile methods should be quite experienced with change. The agile environment in itself operates under a certain level of urgency and uncertainty, both from within and externally. Dalipi, Rufati, and Idrizi (2013) describe the agile environment in terms of the information listed in Table 16.3.

We now describe the type of external and internal levels of uncertainty that can affect the agile project and its environment. Table 16.4 outlines the two categories of uncertainty.

TABLE 16.3

Agile Environments

Agile Environments = [Uncertainty + Unique Expertise] × Speed

Where uncertainties are:

• Internal	=	Under the control of the project manager.
• External	=	Outside the project manager's control.

And:

• Unique expertise	=	Company personnel who possess very broad knowledge and who drive ideas and projects. This also refers to a company's exclusive level of expertise.

And:

• Speed	=	The level of urgency.

Source: Derived from F. Dalipi, E. Rufati, and F. Idrizi. *International Journal of Engineering Research and Development.* 8(3): 20–25, 2013. With permission.

TABLE 16.4

Categories of Agile Project Uncertainty

External	Internal
Changing customer requirements	Technical roadblocks
Competitive actions	Project plan alterations
Changes in industry-specific business setting	
Business plan changes	

Source: Derived from F. Dalipi, E. Rufati, and F. Idrizi. *International Journal of Engineering Research and Development.* 8(3): 20–25, 2013. With permission.

Nonstop Risk Management

In Chapter 10, we discussed risk management as an important part of agile methods. In this chapter, we describe risk management's importance to change management. We wish to reiterate that agile methods are value- and risk-focused. The agile project must always be focused on addressing high-risk and high-priority items simultaneously. We now describe an agile risk management process that can be used for other project types as well (Dalipi et al., 2013).

- Identify risks
- Assess risks
- Create risk response plans
- Reassess the risk throughout the project

As a result of agility, risks can be identified in a single iteration and then mitigated or eliminated in the upcoming iteration. This is the same for positive risks; opportunities can be added to the product backlog as changes that increase the client's competitive advantage. This means that agile methods identify risks prior to their having an impact on the project as a whole. Let's say, for example, that a work item has a low priority. In the event that the item presents itself as a risk, it is then reprioritized as a high-priority item. All risk items are considered to be of high priority even if they were originally designated as low priority. Risk items are moved to the high-priority "basket" as soon as they are discovered and a solution has been found to address their impact. This is another way that changes are handled on the agile project. Risk items and those with high-priority levels are the only candidates for change management on the agile project. To be clear, if a product feature adds value for the customer and is approved, this type of item is given a high priority and is included.

CHAPTER SUMMARY

This concludes our discussion on agile change management. Keep in mind that this process is not an extra one. This process occurs during the maintenance of the product backlog which makes it agile inclusive.

17

Additional Agile Methods

This chapter provides a discussion of additional agile methods that were not covered in Chapter 3. In order to make a determination as to which methods are actually agile, the first fact is that agile methods are adaptive. On the other side of the coin are those methods that are predictive. The differences between these two types of methods determine when to describe a process as agile. All agile methods are adaptive. This means that the method is flexible and allows for changes. Predictive methods, on the other hand, are centered on planning and are concerned with addressing the most serious changes that need to be approved through a configuration control board (CCB). Adaptive methods accept all changes that add value. In addition, agile methods are always going to be iterative or incremental. In addition to the agile characteristics we just described, the following are additional agile buzzwords that are briefly discussed:

- *Cooperative:* This term refers to customer and developer interactions.
- *Straightforward:* This term suggests that the agile method is easy to understand and modify, and that the methodology has been adequately documented.

We now begin our discussion of additional agile methods not previously addressed.

DYNAMIC SYSTEMS DEVELOPMENT METHOD (DSDM)

The DSDM* is considered to be a systems development method that is vigorous in nature. This method was developed by a United Kingdom (UK)

---

* DSDM Consortium. (n.d.)

association in 1994. The basic ideas behind the method are that rather than fixing the amount of functionality in a product and then adjusting time and resources to obtain that functionality, a better approach is to fix time and resources and then adjust the amount of functionality as necessary. Did we all get that? DSDM originated from rapid application development (RAD) and was at one time classified as the first real agile method. The DSDM is defined as an agile project management and delivery framework. This methodology is designed for tailoring and can be used with traditional methods such as PRINCE2.* In addition, DSDM is used to complement other agile methods such as Scrum. The idea behind DSDM is that projects should be lined up with concise, definite strategic goals. The focus of this method is early delivery of tangible benefits to an organization. This method is not vendor dependent and it includes an entire project life cycle. In addition, DSDM includes best practice guidance so that projects can be delivered on time and within budget. The method is scalable and addresses projects of all sizes and any business segment. DSDM supports the use of proven agile techniques including:

- Facilitated workshops
- Modeling and iterative development
- MoSCoW prioritization scheme
- Time-boxing

DSDM is based on nine principles:

1. Active user involvement is imperative.
2. DSDM teams must be empowered to make decisions.
3. The focus is on frequent delivery of products.
4. Fitness for business purpose is the essential criterion for acceptance of deliverables.
5. Iterative and incremental development is necessary to converge on an accurate business solution.
6. All changes during development are reversible.
7. Requirements are baselined at a high level.
8. Testing is integrated throughout the life cycle.
9. This method believes in the Pareto principle (80–20 rule): 80% of an application can be delivered in 20% of the time it would take to deliver 100% of the application. Only enough work should be done in each increment to facilitate movement to the next increment.

---

* PRojects IN Controlled Environments.

TABLE 17.1

Family of Crystal Methods

	Clear	**Yellow**	**Orange**	**Red**	**Maroon**
Life (L)	L6	L20	L40	L80	L200
Essential money (E)	E6	E20	E40	E80	E200
Discretionary money (D)	D6	D20	D40	D80	D200
Comfort (C)	C6	C20	C40	C80	C200
Size	1–6	7–20	21–40	41–80	81–200

CRYSTAL METHODS

The Crystal family is inclusive of several different methods that can be chosen based on being the best match for a project. The methods include practices that can be used for tailoring to fit the changing conditions of diverse projects. The participants of the Crystal family are associated with a color that reflects the weight of the methods. The proper color for a project is based on its size and level of criticality. Bigger projects may require more direction and weightier methods as opposed to smaller ones. The family of Crystal methods can be used for any type of development exercise, tools, or work products. These methods are also open to integrating with other agile methods such as XP and Scrum practices. The family of Crystal methods is described in Table 17.1.

AGILE MODELING (AM)

According to Ambler (2014a), Agile modeling (AM) is a methodology that is practice-based for modeling and documenting software systems. The method supports best practices such as:

1. *Test-driven development (TDD).* A single test should be written at the requirements or the design level. After that, write just enough code to satisfy that test. TDD is a just-in-time (JIT) approach for detailed requirements and the approach is used to confirm for testing.
2. *Model storming.* Model storming is done throughout an iteration on a JIT basis and only for a few minutes in order to explore details about a requirement or to investigate a design issue.

3. *Active stakeholder participation.* Stakeholders must provide information, make decisions in a timely manner, and be actively engaged during the development process through the use of inclusive tools and techniques.

4. *Iteration modeling.* During the beginning of the iterations, some modeling should be done as part of iteration planning activities.

5. *Requirements envisioning.* The scope needs to be established and prioritized requirements need to be created at the beginning of the agile project.

6. *Prioritized requirements.* The requirements are implemented by the agile team in the priority order that has been defined by the project stakeholders. This is done to provide the greatest return on investment (ROI).

7. *Just barely good enough.* A model or documentation should be sufficient for the circumstance at hand and nothing more.

8. *Architecture envisioning.* During the beginning of the agile project, a high-level initial architectural model is necessary in order to identify a viable technical strategy for the solution.

9. *Executable specifications.* Requirements should be specified in terms of an executable customer test. The design should be executable developer tests rather than nonexecutable static documentation.

10. *Document late.* Deliverable documentation should be written as late as possible in order to avoid speculative ideas that will probably change in favor of static information.

11. *Multiple models.* Every type of model has specific strengths and weaknesses. Developers need a range of models in their toolkits that will enable them to apply the correct model in the best manner for the circumstances at hand.

12. *Document continuously.* Deliverable documentation should be written throughout the project life cycle at the same time as the building of the rest of the solution.

13. *Lookahead modeling.* In the event of high-priority requirements that appear to be complex, this would be the motivation to put in the effort for exploratory time prior to these items reaching the top of the stack so that overall risk is reduced.

14. *Single source information.* This is a requirement of the method to capture information only in one place.

TABLE 17.2

Core and Supplementary Agile Modeling Principles

Core Principles	Supplementary Principles
Assume simplicity	Content is more important than representation
Embrace change	Open and honest communication
Enable the next effort as your secondary goal	
Incremental change	
Maximize stakeholder ROI	
Model with purpose	
Multiple models	
Quality work	
Rapid feedback	
Working software is the primary goal	
Travel light	

In other words, this method is an approach used to perform modeling activities. AM tries to adapt modeling practices by using agile as its foundation. The main focus of AM is modeling practices and social values. The underlying idea is to motivate developers to build amply radical models that support design and documentation requirements. Agile modeling also supports the creation of small quantities of models and documentation. Cultural issues are addressed by encouraging communication and methods to establish team configurations and techniques of working.

In addition, agile modeling endorses core and supplementary principles as identified in Table 17.2. Finally, agile modeling supports core and supplementary practices as identified in Table 17.3.

LEAN DEVELOPMENT

Lean development[*] was originally derived from Lean manufacturing based on the Toyota Production System (TPS) at Toyota Motor Corporation. The method's goal is to deliver the maximum amount of value to the customer in the shortest amount of time while providing the highest quality and

---

[*] Leffingwell, LLC and Pearson Education, Inc. (2014)

TABLE 17.3

Agile Modeling Core and Supplementary Practices

Core Practices	Supplementary Practices
Active stakeholder participation	Apply modeling standards
Apply the right artifact(s)	Apply patterns gently
Collective ownership	Discard temporary models
Create several models in parallel	Formalize contract models
Create simple content	Update only when it hurts
Depict models simply	
Display models publicly	
Iterate to another artifact	
Model in small increments	
Model with others	
Prove it with code	
Single source information	
Use the simplest tools	

value to the customer, people, and society. Does most of this sound familiar? You bet it does! The way that the Lean development method intends to meet its goals is to attain continuous flow, isolate interruptions and activities that don't add value, and by consistently decreasing or eliminating obstacles. There are seven principles behind Lean:

1. Eliminate waste
2. Amplify learning
3. Decide as late as possible
4. Deliver as fast as possible
5. Empower the team
6. Build integrity in
7. See the whole

ADAPTIVE SOFTWARE DEVELOPMENT (ASD)

Adaptive software development (ASD)* attempts to bring into play a new way of viewing software development within a business by promoting an adaptive standard. ASD provides solutions for the development of very

---

* University of Missouri-St. Louis. (n.d.)

big and multifaceted systems. This method supports incremental and iterative software development using continuous prototyping. In addition, this method was created from a method known as radical software development. ASD asserts that it provides a framework which has sufficient guidance to keep projects from getting in disarray. On the other hand, the framework's preventive methods don't prohibit development and creativity.

ASD grew from rapid application development (RAD). It is based on the principle of continuous adaption of the process to the "work at hand." The process adaption then becomes the normal state of affairs. Say what? ASD has four phases:

1. *Communication and planning:* This phase includes the preparation of the project specs and proposal documents. In addition, project feasibility and risk assessment documents are prepared.
2. *Analysis:* This phase begins when the customer approves the proposal from the first phase. The quality of the software is documented and approved. Comprehensive information and requirements are gathered by an analyst and the software requirement specifications (SRS) are created.
3. *Design and development:* The adaptive software development process utilizes a prototype approach to verify the design and the requirements.
4. *Testing and deployment:* Test cases are created at the start of this phase for each increment. Modules are unit tested followed by integration testing of the modules. System testing is conducted next, followed by acceptance testing, which is the final test that verifies increments by the customer. Deployment activities include installation, training, and security.

KANBAN

The Toyota Production System (TPS) uses a production control method called the Kanban system. This method has also been referred to as the *Supermarket Method* because the idea was copied from supermarkets. Bulk retailing stores, such as supermarkets, use product control cards to store product information. Toyota utilizes Kanban signs in their production processes and this is how the method originated. Whenever a process

TABLE 17.4

Kanban Production System at Toyota

Production Instruction Kanban	Parts Retrieval Kanban
Step 1: Production instruction Kanban A is removed when an operator retrieves parts.	Step 1: The parts retrieval Kanban is removed when an operator uses parts.
Step 2: Only the exact number of parts indicated on the Kanban are produced.	Step 2: The operator carries the Kanban to retrieve replacement parts.
Step 3: The Kanban is attached to the newly produced parts, ready for the next process.	Step 3: The operator removes the production instruction Kanban and replaces it with parts retrieval Kanban.
	Step 4: Parts displaying the parts retrieval Kanban are transported to the next process.

at Toyota mentions a previous process to retrieve automotive parts, it will use a Kanban to communicate that those parts have been used. There are two types of Kanban that are used for managing parts at Toyota: production instruction Kanban and parts retrieval Kanban. Table 17.4 provides the steps to both processes. Oh, by the way, *Kanban* means signboard.

Just-In-Time (JIT)

The just-in-time* slogan refers to producing "only what is needed, when it is needed, and in the amount needed." In order to be effective when producing a large number of cars, the requirement is to create a detailed production plan that includes parts. The idea to supply only what is needed, when it is needed, and in the amount needed, characterizes a method that can eliminate waste, discrepancies, and irrational requirements. This will result in overall value-added productivity levels.

RAPID PRODUCT DEVELOPMENT (RPD)

RPD[†] is a collection of methods that use state-of-the-art engineering practices that rely on short, iterative development cycles that offer potentially high-quality products that are cost efficient and are able to stand up to

---

* Toyota Motor Corporaton (2014)
† Bullinger et al. (2000)

today's tough competitive pressures. During product research, the effort is on both the product and the development process. The idea is to pursue several alternatives within contemporary methods so that the best solution can be found. RPD is a methodology that pools all influences (organizational configuration, process, assets, and the product development process) of the engineering process to an iterative development. The method uses multiple prototypes to assist with the realization of early and cost-effective evaluations of varied options.

As a result of a shortened positioning cycle of new products entering the marketplace, it has been crucial for companies to develop groundbreaking products rather quickly. Creating prototypes is very important for a rapid product development process. RPD is an organizational model that designates a rapid development process that is attained by uniting and integrating prototyping technology into the research and development (R&D) process. The method has the following objectives:

- Shorten the time to market.
- Develop groundbreaking products by optimizing time, cost, and quality factors.
- Increase quality based on the logic of the principle of comprehensiveness.

The RPD process is initiated by the developments in the marketplace, lawmaking, or new technologies. R&D management is required in order to address uncertainties, especially in cases where the customer changes the requirements late in the project. The RPD's life cycle is not required to be sequential because the idea behind an evolutionary design suggests that unrecognized requirements or progress should be considered and added. This action is an important feature of RPD: the relinquishment of a similar description of a product throughout the project. Following is a description of the elements of RPD:

1. *Physical prototypes:* Prototypes are important factors that support product design and process planning. Prototypes can show how far requirements are satisfied. In addition, they assist with helping to learn quickly, lessen the number of mistakes, and help with the integration of different functions. Technical and functional prototypes are very important tools used to speed up the development process.

2. *Digital prototypes:* As a result of physical prototypes being costly and time consuming, a virtual prototype during the early phases of product development enhances the entire development process. A clear advantage of digital prototyping is the progression from the testing phase with physical prototypes to the early phases of product development with digital prototypes. A digital demo permits early modifications and optimization of the prototype and cost savings. Also, a virtual prototype can be verified rather easily, resulting in the reduction of development time.

In summary, the physical or virtual prototypes of the system are very important during the product development process. The use of prototypes provides structure and a disciplined approach that improves the level of learning and integration within the development process.

FEATURE-DRIVEN DEVELOPMENT (FDD)

Feature-driven development (FDD) is a process-focused software development method used for creating business critical systems. The method's approach is centered on its design and construction phases. FDD symbolizes iterative development and uses practices that are realized to be industry effective. The blend of its methods makes for its processes to be unique for every case where the method is applied. Quality features are highlighted throughout the method's processes, including frequent delivery and precise project monitoring. There are five iterative phases in the life cycle for FDD:

1. *Develop an overall model:* An object model plus notes
2. *Build a features list:* A list of features grouped into sets and subject area
3. *Plan by feature:* A development plan; class owners; feature set owners
4. *Design by feature:* A design package
5. *Build by feature:* Complete client functionality

FUTURE IMPLICATIONS FOR AGILE METHODS

Based on a study conducted by Abrahamsson et al. (2003), there are several implications uncovered that affect the future of these methods. Even though this particular study was done more than 10 years ago; the author of this book believes that the implications from the study continue to have merit.

Project Management

Support for project management in many of the agile methods is either scarce or does not exist. Project management is very important when agile practices are adhered to such as daily build, short releases, and the like. In addition, it is apparent that release and build activities are very different from one method to another and this has the potential for confusion. Project managers can be in a tricky position when decisions need to be made with regard to deciding upon the most suitable methods to use. The success of any agile method is dependent upon it being included in the project's daily pace. Research has shown that some developers purposely use different terminology in order to secure their niche. Therefore it is imperative that project management activities be addressed so the developer and project management goals can be in synch.

Software Development Life Cycles

Research has revealed that different agile methods cover very different phases of the software development life cycle. No rationalization was presented for the reasons behind the missing lifecycle phases. Software development methods are required to be "complete" rather than partial. The debate is whether to add more phases in order to be extensive or whether a decision should be made to cover less in order to be more precise. The deciding factor is, of course, the associated costs; however, no method was identified to be either precise or extensive. Some agile practitioners have come up with half-baked solutions that in actuality cover a wider range than the actual methods. A proposition was made for the developers to focus more on being specialists rather than generalists in their knowledge areas. The actual issue at hand now boils down to two considerations:

1. Methods that cover too much may be too broad or superficial for use.
2. Methods that cover too little may be too constrained or lack an association to other methods.

Abstract Principles versus Concrete Guidance

Research has shown that only a third of the agile methods provide concrete guidance. The agile principles appear to be very abstract. The evidence is that agilists are more concerned with getting acceptance of the values rather than offering guidance on how to put the values into actual use. The research revealed that guidance only exists in those methods which are restricted in scope. The conclusion is that more work is required to determine how the practice, work products, and the like can be used in different companies so that practitioners can obtain a solid foundation on which to base their decisions.

Universally Predefined versus Situation Appropriate

Research has revealed that some of the popular agile methods were detected to be commonly predefined. Crystal methods and a few others acknowledge the fact that a single method does not fit all circumstances. As a result of these findings, upcoming methods and such should focus on situational suitability and provide guidance on how the agile methods could be used in different capacities. This would include the capability to identify the conditions where adjustment activities need to take place.

Empirical Support

Research has shown that empirical evidence is very scarce. Only a mere third of the methods use empirical support for the claims that they make. On the other hand, some of the agile methods are increasing the number of empirical studies which should mature the methodological foundation of the methods. In addition, lack of such empirical evidence results in agilists not having dependable evidence regarding the usefulness of the method.

CHAPTER SUMMARY

Agile methods provide an alternative approach to traditional project management procedures. Agile methods have been developed to enable business to respond to uncertainty. Globally, agile methods have been embraced, however, some organizations need assistance during the transition process. In order to embrace these methods effectively, training, change in mindset, and cultural transformation may be required. However, the world as we used to see it has become more unquestionably "agile."

18

Starting Your Agile Journey

The agile journey begins with embracing change. For many organizations, moving to agile is going to be a change from the waterfall methodology. For many individuals, the move to agile will undoubtedly imply a shift in mindset and comfort level. The author recommends (and many will not be comfortable with this) to just jump in and "do it!" This would be after the proper research and analysis is done that supports the just "do it" attitude, however. In other words, conduct the proper analysis from Chapter 15 to determine if there are projects on the organization's horizon that are agile candidates and if there are, just "do it!" Is this simple enough? Probably not for many but it's a bold way to get started. For those individuals and organizations that are very cautious (and cautious is not a bad thing at all), the author provides several guidelines for getting started with your agile journey.

STARTING THE AGILE JOURNEY AS AN INDIVIDUAL

The first step to begin your journey as an individual should be with training. There is no better way to get the knowledge you need than to get formal training. Chapter 13 provided a list of many popular agile certifications that require training. In fact, all of the certifications listed in Chapter 13 require training that can be used to obtain the related certification described in that chapter. How cool is that? So basically, an individual can kill two birds with one stone by obtaining the required training for the certification and then getting agile certified. There is no better way. Is this simple enough? The author believes so. To summarize: review Chapter 13, decide on a certification, take the training, and then get certified. The question now becomes, "How would one decide on which credential is the best one for you as an individual?" That would be a personal decision that only the candidate can make; however, the author does believe that credentials from the Project Management Institute (PMI) are highly desired. Did the author just recommend the PMI? Indeed! So now there you have it. All that is needed now is to just do it! Is there more? For those of you who don't have the experience required by the PMI, you won't be left out in the cold. There are other registered education providers (REPs) that provide training and certifications for those who lack formal experience and Chapter 13 has provided the details. So what are you waiting for? The author has provided what you need to get started, so go for it.

STARTING THE AGILE JOURNEY AS AN ORGANIZATION

First of all, an organization needs to understand why they may have no choice about moving to agile. A business may be left behind if it takes too long to move its products and services to market. Agile organizations are increasing profits and market shares because they are pleasing their customers faster than others. In contrast, companies that are slow to change with market conditions are often at a disadvantage and may end up going out of business if they are not able to keep up. According to InfoQ (2012), take the STEP (Stop, Transform, Expand, and Perfect) toward the move to agility.

Stop

Organizations need to "stop" and start to evaluate different ways to work. Once these methods are identified and established, they should be supported within the organization on a regular basis. With regard to agility, leaders should share its benefits with all so that there is a strong inspiration for others in the organization to want to learn more about these methods. The agile organizational journey most often begins with a continuous improvement thought process.

Transform

As upper management and agile practitioners in an organization begin to embrace agile methods wholeheartedly, it will be important for them to develop a shared understanding of where the improvement methods can be best applied. Quite often, an organization seeking ways to keep value flowing to their customers consider agile methods as a way to remove restrictions from their existing business processes. As these restrictions are removed, processes become repeatable and progressively affect improvement throughout an entire system. It should be cautioned that changing the organizational culture is not expected to occur overnight. A better approach is to begin with small changes, such as establishing a small number of cross-functional, self-organizing agile teams. This gives the organization sufficient time to engage its leadership in gaining understanding of the impediments that affect the cycle time of its product development processes. The transformation to agile should be gradual, with only a few individuals at a time. During this time, metrics should be captured that support process improvements, and there will be improvements.

Expand

After the creation of a few agile teams who should be provided with coaching and training support, the expectation is that the organization can now confidently begin to influence the organizational culture. This should be done with the utilization of agile champions within the organization who can begin to create full-blown mentoring programs and interest groups. This is necessary so that the knowledge obtained by the agile teams can be spread throughout the organization and potentially even across its borders. Although there is the perception that agile methods are project based, organizations need to understand that agility can be used to inspire the usage of practices and techniques that teams can use to improve their workflows. Improvement in work processes across an organization can be extremely beneficial and maintaining a culture of continuous improvement is the place to start.

An organization can expect a more predictable operating capacity as the agile teams increase their velocities. Forecasting is expected to be much more accurate, based on more accurate historical records. Statistical analysis will then be in a better position to guide continuous improvement activities and strategic initiatives will become increasingly more reliable.

The organization can also expect to see improvements in program and portfolio planning. By using agile as opposed to traditional methods, management can focus on planning with fixed budgets and deciding on how many agile teams they need to utilize for certain product release initiatives. Product scope is established based upon the greatest amount of customer value and features are combined into small product increments and released as quickly as possible.

Perfect

In the agile world or any part of the world, organizations should understand that a perfect process that will guarantee success does not exist. There are, however, processes that contribute to "customer delight." In order for the organization to master customer delight on a consistent basis, it must engage in a long journey of continuous improvement. In order to delight customers over and over again, the organization must understand the needs of each of its customers. Only through such understanding can organizations come up with new ideas to delight its customers. The agile team was designed to keep delighting the customer by determining new ways to make work satisfying on all levels. The most effective agile teams are those that reflect on ways to remove impediments, scrutinize their processes, and find ways for innovation and continuous improvements. These teams are excited about their agile journey and are constantly finding ways to work better and smarter. All they did was to take the STEP. Are you ready to take yours? Just do it!

References

CHAPTER 1

Griffiths, M. (2012). *PMI-ACP Exam Prep.* United States: RMC.

Project Management Institute, Inc. (2013). *A Guide to the Project Management Body of Knowledge (PMBOK® Guide),* 5th edition. Newtown Square, PA: PMI.

CHAPTER 2

Griffiths, M. (2012). *PMI-ACP Exam Prep.* United States: RMC.

CHAPTER 3

Admad, G., Soomro, T.R., and Brohi, M.N. (2014). Agile methodologies: Comparative study and future direction. *European Academic Research.* Retrieved from http://www.euacademic.org/UploadArticle/273.pdf

Griffiths, M. (2012). *PMI-ACP Exam Prep.* United States: RMC.

Scrum Alliance. (2013). *Core Scrum-Values and Roles.* Retrieved from http://www.scrumalliance.org/why-scrum/core-scrum-values-roles

SCRUMstudy. (2013). *A Guide to the Scrum Body of Knowledge (SBOK Guide),* 2013 edition. Phoenix, AZ: SCRUMstudy, a brand of VMEdu, Inc.

Wells, D. (2013a). *Extreme Programming—A Gentle Introduction.* Retrieved from http://www.extremeprogramming.org/rules/pair.html

Wells, D. (2013b). *Extreme Programming—The Values of Extreme Programming.* Retrieved from http://www.extremeprogramming.org/values.html

CHAPTER 4

Agile Alliance. (2014). *Task Board.* Agile Alliance. Retrieved from http://guide.agilealliance.org/guide/taskboard.html

Azizyan, G., Magarian, M., and Kajko-Mattsson, M. (2012). The dilemma of tool selection for agile project management. *ICSEA 2012: The Seventh International Conference on Software Engineering Advances.* Retrieved from http://www.thinkmind.org/index.php?view=article&articleid=icsea_2012_21_40_10376

Griffiths, M. (2012). *PMI-ACP Exam Prep.* United States: RMC.

CHAPTER 5

Agile Alliance. (2014). *Invest.* Retrieved from http://guide.agilealliance.org/guide/invest.html

Griffiths, M. (2012). *PMI-ACP Exam Prep.* United States: RMC.

Project Management Institute, Inc. (2013). *A Guide to the Project Management Body of Knowledge (PMBOK® Guide),* 5th edition. Newtown Square, PA: PMI.

CHAPTER 6

Ambler, S. (2012a). *Agile Modeling: Best Practices for Agile/Lean Documentation*. Retrieved from http://www.agilemodeling.com/essays/agileDocumentationBestPractices.htm

Ambler, S. (2012b). *Agile Modeling Principles (AM) v2*. Retrieved from http://www.agilemodeling.com/principles.htm#QualityWork

CHAPTER 7

Agile Alliance. (2014). *Agile Project Reporting and Metrics*. Retrieved from http://www.scrumalliance.org/community/articles/2013/july/agile-project-reporting-and-metrics

Griffiths, M. (2012). *PMI-ACP: Exam Prep*. United States: RMC.

Project Management Institute, Inc. (2013). *A Guide to the Project Management Body of Knowledge (PMBOK® Guide)*, 5th edition. Newtown Square, PA: PMI.

CHAPTER 8

Ambysoft, Inc. (2013). *Agile Data: Development Sandboxes: An Agile 'Best Practice.'* Retrieved from http://www.agiledata.org/essays/sandboxes.html

Griffiths, M. (2012). *PMI-ACP: Exam Prep*. United States: RMC.

Jalic, Inc. (2014). *The Literature Network: The Elephant's Child*. Retrieved from http://www.online-literature.com/poe/165/

Kipling, R. (1902). *Rudyard Kipling Quotes*. Retrieved from http://www.goodreads.com/author/quotes/6989.Rudyard_Kipling?page=4

Leffingwell, LLC. (2014a). *Scaled Agile Framework: Agile Team Abstract*. Retrieved from http://scaledagileframework.com/agile-teams/

Leffingwell, LLC. (2014b). *Scaled Agile Framework: Spikes Abstract*. Retrieved from http://scaledagileframework.com/spikes/

MathisFun. (2013). *Fibonacci Sequence*. Retrieved from http://www.mathsisfun.com/numbers/fibonacci-sequence.html

Project Management Institute, Inc. (2013). *A Guide to the Project Management Body of Knowledge (PMBOK® Guide)*, 5th edition. Newtown Square, PA: PMI.

Scott Ambler & Associates. (2012). *Agile Modeling: Introduction to Agile Usability*. Retrieved from http://www.agilemodeling.com/essays/agileUsability.htm

Scrum Alliance. (2013). *An Agile Process for User Acceptance Testing*. Retrieved from https://www.scrumalliance.org/community/articles/2013/july/an-agile-process-for-user-acceptance-testing

SCRUMstudy. (2013). *A Guide to the Scrum Body of Knowledge (SBOK™ Guide)*, 2013 edition. Phoenix, AZ: SCRUMstudy, a brand of VMEdu, Inc.

CHAPTER 9

Griffiths, M. (2012). *PMI-ACP: Exam Prep*. United States: RMC.

CHAPTER 10

Project Management Institute, Inc. (2013). *A Guide to the Project Management Body of Knowledge (PMBOK® Guide)*, 5th edition. Newtown Square, PA: PMI.

CHAPTER 11

Greenleaf, R.K. (1991, 2008). *The Servant as Leader*. Westfield, IN: The Greenleaf Center for Servant Leadership.

Griffiths, M. (2012). *PMI-ACP: Exam Prep*. United States: RMC.

Project Management Institute, Inc. (2013). *A Guide to the Project Management Body of Knowledge (PMBOK® Guide)*, 5th edition. Newtown Square, PA: PMI.

SCRUMstudy. (2013). *A Guide to the Scrum Body of Knowledge (SBOK™ Guide)*, 2013 edition. Phoenix, AZ: SCRUMstudy, a brand of VMEdu, Inc.

CHAPTER 12

Griffiths, M. (2012). *PMI-ACP: Exam Prep*. United States: RMC.

Innovation Games. (2013a). *Innovation Games—Me and My Shadow*. Retrieved from http://www.innovationgames.com/me-and-my- shadow/

Innovation Games. (2013b). *Innovation Games—Product Box*. Retrieved from http://www.innovationgames.com/product-box/

Innovation Games. (2013c). *Innovation Games—Start Your Day*. Retrieved from http://www.innovationgames.com/start-your-day/

Leffingwell, LLC. (2014). *Agile Teams Extract*. Retrieved from http://scaledagileframework.com/agile-teams/

Project Management Institute, Inc. (2013). *A Guide to the Project Management Body of Knowledge (PMBOK® Guide)*, 5th edition. Newtown Square, PA: PMI.

SCRUMstudy. (2013). *A Guide to the Scrum Body of Knowledge (SBOK™ Guide)*, 2013 edition. Phoenix, AZ: SCRUMstudy, a brand of VMEdu, Inc.

CHAPTER 13

PMI. (2014). *PMI Agile Certified Practitioner (PMI-ACP)*. Retrieved from http://www.pmi.org/Certification/New-PMI-Agile-Certification.aspx

Scrum Alliance. (2014a). *Certified ScrumMaster (CSM)*. Retrieved from http://www.scrumalliance.org/certifications/practitioners/certified-scrummaster-(csm)

Scrum Alliance. (2014b). *Certified Scrum Coach (CSC)*. Retrieved from http://www.scrumalliance.org/certifications/csc-certification

Scrum Alliance. (2014c). *Certified Scrum Product Owner (CSPO)*. Retrieved from http://www.scrumalliance.org/certifications/practitioners/cspo-certification

Scrum Alliance. (2014d). *Certified Scrum Developer (CSD)*. Retrieved from http://www.scrumalliance.org/certifications/practitioners/csd-certification

Scrum Alliance. (2014e). *Certified Scrum Professional (CSP)*. Retrieved from http://www.scrumalliance.org/certifications/practitioners/csp-certification

Scrum Alliance. (2014f). *Certified Scrum Trainer (CST)*. Retrieved from http://www.scrumalliance.org/certifications/trainers

SCRUMstudy. (2014a). *Scrum Developer Certified (SDC)*. Retrieved from http://www.SCRUMstudy.com/scrum-developer-certification.asp

SCRUMstudy. (2014b). *Scrum Master Certified (SMC)*. Retrieved from http://www.SCRUMstudy.com/scrum-master-certification.asp

SCRUMstudy. (2014c). *Agile Expert Certified (AEC)*. Retrieved from http://www.SCRUMstudy.com/agile-certification.asp

SCRUMstudy. (2014d). *Scrum Product Owner Certified (SPOC).* Retrieved from http://www.SCRUMstudy.com/scrum-product-owner-certification.asp

SCRUMstudy. (2014e). *Expert ScrumMaster (ESM).* Retrieved from http://www.SCRUMstudy.com/expert-scrum-master-certification.asp

SCRUMstudy. (2014f). *SCRUMstudy Certified Trainer (SCT).* Retrieved from http://www.SCRUMstudy.com/trainer-accreditation-process.asp

CHAPTER 14

Griffiths, M. (2012). *PMI-ACP Exam Prep.* United States: RMC.

Scrum Alliance. (2013). *Agile Contracting: A Story-Point Billing Model.* Retrieved from http://www.scrumalliance.org/community/articles/2013/2013-april/agile-contracting-a-story-point-billing-model

Sutherland, J. (2013). ScrumInc.: *Scrum Log Jeff Sutherland.* Retrieved from http://scrum.jeffsutherland.com/2008/08/agile-2008-money-for-nothing.html

CHAPTER 15

Gandomani, T.J., Zulzalil, H., Ghani, A.A.A., and Sultan, A.B.M. (2013). Towards comprehensive and disciplined change management strategy in agile transformation process. *Research Journal of Applied Sciences, Engineering and Technology,* 6(13): 2345–2351.

Griffiths, M. (2012). *PMI-ACP Exam Prep.* United States: RMC.

Murthy, A. S. (2013). *Agile in Software Projects: Where Does It Fit? Where Doesn't It? What About Hybrid Models?* Newtown Square, PA: PMI Virtual Library.

Rowe, B. (2014). *Culture Shift and Change in Process Can Mean Agile Success for IT Development Projects.* Newtown Square, PA: PMI Virtual Library.

Turk, D., France, R., and Rumpe, B. (2002). Limitations of agile software processes. In *Third International Conference on eXtreme Programming and Agile Processes in Software Engineering.* pp. 43–46.

van Dijk, R.W. (2011). Determining the suitability of agile methods for a software project. In *15th Twente Student Conference on IT.* University of Twente Enschede, The Netherlands, June 20.

Veneziano, V., Rainer, A.W., and Haider, S. (2014). *When Agile Is Not Good Enough: An Initial Attempt at Understanding How to Make the Right Decision.* University of Hertfordshire: School of Computer Science, pp. 1–10.

CHAPTER 16

Ambler, S.W. (2014). *Agile Modeling: Agile Requirements Change Management.* Retrieved from http://www.agilemodeling.com/essays/changeManagement.htm

Dalipi, F., Rufati, E., and Idrizi, F. (2013). Applying agile software development methodology in a dynamic business environment. *International Journal of Engineering Research and Development,* 8(3): 20–25.

CHAPTER 17

Abrahamsson, P., Warsta, J., Siponen, M.T., and Ronkainen, J. (2003). New Directions on Agile Methods: A Comparative Analysis. Proceedings of the 25th International Conference on Software Engineering, Portland, OR, May 3–10, pp. 244–254. IEEE.

Ambler, S. (2014a). *Agile Modeling (AM) Home Page: Effective Practices for Modeling and Documentation.* Retrieved from http://agilemodeling.com/

Ambler, S. (2014b). *Agile Modeling: Feature Driven Development and Agile Modeling.* Retrieved from http://www.agilemodeling.com/essays/fdd.htm

Bullinger, H.-J., Warschat, J., and Fischer, D. (2000). Rapid product development—An overview. *Computers in Industry,* 42(2000): 99–108. Elsevier.

DSDM Consortium. (n.d.). *What Is DSDM?* Retrieved from http://www.dsdm.org/content/what-dsdm

Leffingwell, LLC. and Pearson Education, Inc. (2014). *Lean Abstract.* Retrieved from http://scaledagileframework.com/lean/

Toyota Motor Corporation. (2014). *Just-in-Time: Philosophy of Complete Elimination of Waste.* Retrieved from http://www.toyota-global.com/company/vision_philosophy/toyota_production_system/just-in-time.html

University of Missouri-St. Louis. (n.d.). *Agile Methodologies.* Retrieved from http://www.umsl.edu/~sauterv/analysis/6840_f09_papers/Nat/Agile.html

CHAPTER 18

InfoQ. (2012). *STEP—A Map for an Agile Journey.* Retrieved from http://www.infoq.com/articles/STEP-map-Agile-Journey

Index

Note: Page numbers ending in "f" refer to figures. Page numbers ending in "t" refer to tables.

for agile, 51–60
concerns of, 54–55, 55t
controlling, 52
ensuring, 55–56
explanation of, 51–53
management concepts, 51–56
Stakeholder groups, 52–55, 55t
Stakeholder management
concepts of, 51–56
concerns of, 54–55, 55t
ensuring, 55–56
people for, 53
plans for, 52
traditional management, 51–53
vendor management, 54–55
Stakeholder techniques
agile modeling, 57
communications management, 58
information displays, 59
personas, 57
user stories, 58
website wireframes, 57–58
Stakeholder tools. *See also* Tools
agile modeling, 57
communications management, 58
information displays, 59
overview of, 56–57
personas, 57
user stories, 58
website wireframes, 57–58
Statements of work (SOW), 160
Static documentation, 62–63, 190
STEP (Stop, Transform, Expand, Perfect),
202–203
Stories, 58, 90, 98–99, 99t. *See* User stories
Story maps, 88–89
Story point billing model, 156–158
Story points technique, 69–73, 71f, 83–86
Sustainable pace, 4, 14, 39, 53, 83

T

Tailoring concept, 105–106
Task boards
benefits of, 69–70
for delivering value, 106–107
explanation of, 50
user stories on, 69–70, 70f
for WIP, 74–75

Teams
aligning, 136–137
characteristics of, 129–131
coaching, 137
collaboration, 132–133
commitment, 135
communication, 134
definition of, 129–130
formation stages, 125, 125t
games, 133–134
leadership skills, 123–127, 125t
magic of, 131–135
motivating, 135–136
problem detection, 138–140
problem resolution, 137
responsibilities of, 82–83
Scrum of Scrums, 135–136, 136f
Scrum team, 29–31
size of, 135–136, 136f
team velocity, 34–37, 43, 59, 70, 71f,
91–94, 134
traditional teams, 130–131, 131t
Test-driven development (TDD), 39–40,
47–48, 62, 62f, 94, 97, 189
Tests
acceptance test-driven development,
47–48, 96–97
acceptance tests, 47–48, 96–97, 140
automated testing, 97
test cases, 97
test-driven development, 39–40,
47–48, 62, 62f, 94, 97, 189
Time-boxing
commitments and, 135
constraints of, 82
dynamic systems development
method, 187–188
explanation of, 22–23, 28
iteration planning and, 94
for meetings, 23–24, 28, 31–32, 56,
99–100, 138
Scrum planning and, 31–32
teams and, 136–137
Tools
analysis of, 44–47, 46t
attributes of, 45t, 46t
automated tools, 47–48
build tools, 48, 140
cameras, 49